America's Favorite Quilts

Also by Leslie Linsley

America's Favorite Quilts

Leslie Linsley

Delacorte Press/New York

America's Favorite Quilts

Preparation and design:	Jon Aron Studio
Art direction:	Jon Aron
Illustrations:	Michael Strahm Jeffrey Terr
Research:	Amy Brunhuber
Photography:	O. E. Nelson

Published by
Delacorte Press
1 Dag Hammarskjold Plaza
New York, N.Y. 10017

Manufactured in the United States of America

First printing

Library of Congress Cataloging in Publication Data
Linsley, Leslie.
America's favorite quilts.
Includes index.
1. Quilting — United States — Patterns.   I. Title.
TT835.L56 1983   746.9′7041′0973   83-5138
ISBN 0-385-29268-6

This book is dedicated to Hester Phreaner
for her friendship and inspiration.

The quilts presented in this book are from
the collection of Joanna S. Rose.

Contents

Introduction

I grew up in an old house in Connecticut where every room held something quilted. A pillow on the rocking chair, a lap throw on the couch, and, of course, a quilt on every bed. Quilt names like Log Cabin, Wedding Ring, and Lone Star were as familiar to me as my own name, and I thought every household counted quilted coverlets among its possessions. It was a surprise to find that many of my friends slept under plain wool blankets and missed the joys of finding recycled patches from old clothes on their bedcovers.

Now my children sleep under Dresden Plates and modern versions of familiar patchwork designs that my mother has created for them. And when one of my daughter's cherished Wedding Ring quilts finally became too shredded for repair, we cut up all the good parts to make into pillows.

Today, the whole country is quilt-conscious, but quiltmaking has been part of America's way of life since our country was first settled. Initially, patchwork and appliqué were done as a necessity to keep warm, and the thrifty North American settlers pieced together scraps of fabric from worn-out clothing. Later, making patchworks became a social event, a means of socializing while being productive during cold winter nights. The history of our American way of life was stitched into those early quilts at quilting bees where patterns and gossip were exchanged. Block patterns evolved from simple shapes that reflected an entirely new meaning in needlework design.

Only one form of needlework is our own American folk art and that is our pieced patchwork, the sewing together of fabric to fabric to create a pieced whole cloth. To the women who made our earliest quilts, every scrap of fabric took on a new importance. They began to look at the pieces with an eye to seeing what simple shapes could be created from them. From such shapes as an orange peel, turkey tracks in the snow, a rose growing in the garden, or a log cabin, American women developed pieced and appliquéd patterns that are still cherished, copied, revised, reproduced, and faithfully restored today.

In the last decade there has been a renewed interest in American folk art. We see now that the simple elegance of the geometric designs of patchwork quilts has an amazingly contemporary look even when placed in a traditional setting. The colors are basic, the designs bold. The graphic quality of early quilts has inspired modern quilt lovers to use them as wall hangings rather than bed coverings. This idea might perplex early quiltmakers, but perhaps not. They were well aware of the special qualities of this craftwork.

In the old days the pieced quilt was considered to be less important in status than the elaborately quilted or appliquéd quilt. Today these patchwork quilts, mostly done between 1750 and 1850, are among the most prized because of their wonderful designs. Time adds significance to a quilt.

When researching this book, I spoke with many quiltmakers in various parts of the country and I received hundreds of photographs showing examples of the excellent needlework and sense of design of modern quiltmakers. The interviews, letters, and photographs indicate as well the strong interest people have in reinterpreting the old, and still favorite, familiar patterns.

The quilt collection here represents twenty-seven of America's favorite designs. Since these are antique quilts you can see in many of them idiosyncrasies in the craftwork or imperfections in the design as well as signs of the wear and tear of time. The limitation of fabrics and the fading and softening of colors adds to the charm of some of them. The color schemes reflect the period and tradition they were made in more than the taste of the quiltmaker.

Before the development of printed fabrics, quilts were often made of only two or three colors such as red and white or red, green, and white. Today, many find satisfaction in re-creating a design exactly, using the exact same colors, but you can also create your own color scheme.

The quilting patterns found on the backgrounds and borders of the quilts are as traditional as the designs. Certain patterns are always found on specific quilts. Once again, when making your own quilts you can follow the authentic, traditional pattern or make up your own combination. The directions we give for making the quilts in this book always follow the original. Only the sizes are modified when necessary.

I think quiltmakers would agree, if you're making just one quilt or embarking on a new hobby that may have you making hundreds, you must start out with a traditionally American design.

While most of us are too busy to commit ourselves to many long leisure-time activities, quilting has much appeal. Perhaps in our hurried lives we can find contentment in reaching back into the past to carry on a tradition. Many of today's quiltmakers feel they are creating future heirlooms. When our children reach into the attic to pass something on to their children, a handmade quilt may be what they'll find. By re-creating the originally conceived patterns, we can keep them alive, thus adding to or becoming part of an American tradition.

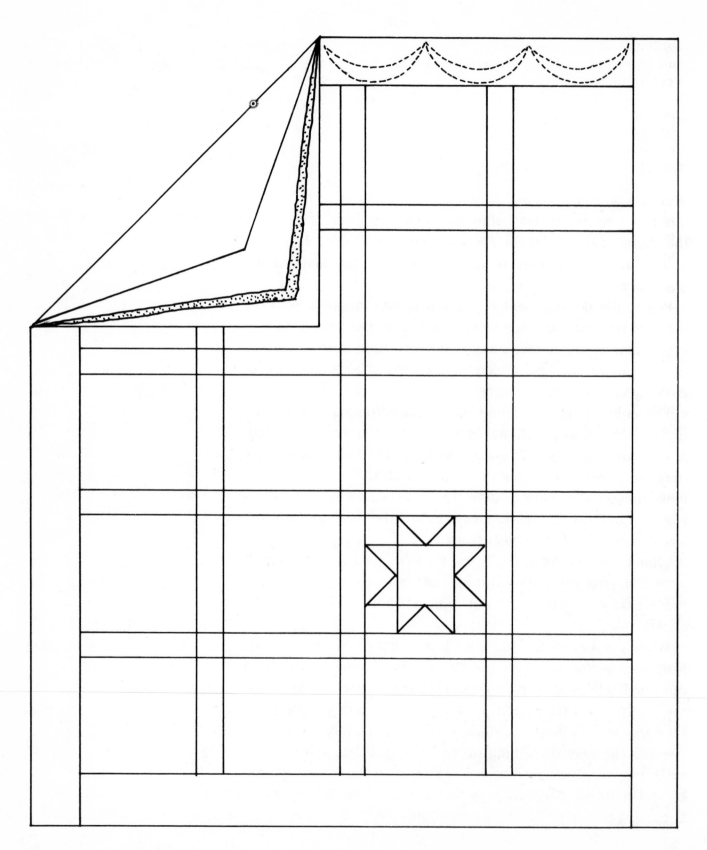

Appliqué: The technique of creating a design by cutting a shape from one fabric and stitching it to a contrasting fabric block.

Backing: The bottom piece of fabric that is of the same weight as the top. This piece can be a solid or printed fabric that matches the design on the top.

Basting: Securing the top, batting, and backing together with long loose stitches before quilting. These stitches are removed as each section is quilted.

Batting: The soft lining that makes the quilt puffy and gives it warmth. A quilt can be made with various thicknesses of batting.

Batts: Pieces of batting.

Binding: The way the raw edges of the quilt are finished. It can be done by cutting the backing slightly larger than the top. This piece is brought forward, turned, and hemmed to the top, creating a finished border. Or the top and back can be turned inward and stitched together. Another binding method is to sew a strip of contrasting fabric around the quilt by machine or hand, or to use a commercial binding tape.

Block: Sometimes referred to as a square. Geometric or symmetrical pieces of fabric are sewn together to create a design. Finished blocks are sewn together, usually with a border (or sash) between each square.

Patchwork: Sewing together of fabric pieces to create an entire design. Sometimes the shapes form a geometric block. The blocks are then sewn together to make up the completed quilt.

Piecing: Joining patchwork pieces together to form a design on the block.

Quilting: Stitching together 2 layers of fabric with a layer of batting between.

Quilting pattern: The lines or markings on the fabric that make up the design. Small hand or machine stitches quilt along these lines, which might be straight or curved or made up of elaborately curlicued patterns.

Sash or strips: The narrow pieces of fabric used to frame the individual blocks and join them together. These are often of a contrasting color.

Setting: Joining the quilt blocks to form the finished top piece of the quilt.

Template: A pattern that is rigid and full size. It can be cut from cardboard or plastic. (It was originally cut from tin.) This is used to trace the design elements. When cutting out the fabric, you will add ¼-inch seam allowance.

Top: The top of a quilt is the front layer of fabric with the right side showing.

Materials for Quiltmaking

Fabric: Fabric is the main concern of the quilt-making process. Most of the quilts shown in the book were made long ago when the choice of fabrics was limited. And traditionally quiltmakers didn't buy fabric especially for quilts but rather used what was on hand. In this way a quilt became a family "documentary" with bits and pieces of worn-out or outgrown clothing cut up and pieced together. Can't you just hear the various members of a family as they pick out a spot of someone's graduation dress or a piece from father's tie or a favorite dress? And the faded, worn look is part of the charm and appeal of the traditional old quilts.

Today we have so many different fabrics, patterns, and colors available that it is more difficult and yet more exciting to plan such a project. If you have been a sewer for many years, you probably have a nice collection of scraps from which a quilt might emerge.

Cotton has always been the most popular fabric for quilts; however, a cotton blend is preferred by many. For best results choose fabrics of the same fiber content.

The colors and patterns of the fabric will greatly affect the quilt design. For example, a combination of light and dark shades helps define the pattern, while similar shades will produce a more flowing and subtle design.

Needles: These are often called "betweens." The sizes most commonly used are #7 and #8 Sharps. An embroidery needle in the same size is also good. It is especially useful for appliqué and piecing.

Thread: Cotton thread is best for appliqué and piecing. There is a special quilting thread that has a coating to make it stronger. Match the thread to the color of the fabric.

Scissors: If you invest in good-quality scissors from the start, they will be the best investment you'll ever make. This is especially true if you plan to continue with this craft. A good pair of scissors can cut a straight line of fabric without fraying or pulling it. Do not use them for anything but cutting fabric. If you cut paper with your fabric scissors, they will not perform as well again.

It's also a good idea to have small snipping scissors handy. These will be invaluable, especially for hand stitching.

Thimble: Not an absolute must, but a definite plus if you can get used to wearing it. I never have, but I'm working on it. If you are making a quilt with hand-sewn stitching, you will be taking 3 to 6 stitches at a time through the 2 layers of fabric and a layer of batting. A thimble will make the work easier, quicker, and less painful.

Templates: Cardboard, such as shirtboard or oaktag, is perfect for cutting templates. Clear plastic is also used (sold in sheets in art-supply stores) because it keeps a clean, crisp edge and you can see through it. In this way you can get an idea about how a piece will look before cutting it out.

Markers: A soft pencil is good for tracing and transferring designs to the fabric. There are water-soluble pens for this purpose as well. You can mark on the fabric, and when the quilt is finished, any marks that show can be easily removed without scrubbing by simply using a plant mister.

Iron: It would be impossible to do any sewing project without an iron at your elbow. Use a steam iron for quick and easy piecing.

Frame or hoop: Most quilting can be done on a large hoop. For many, a full-size quilting frame is essential. The size depends on the project. You will find these in quilting stores or through mail order sources.

Rulers: A yardstick and ruler are needed. A clear plastic ruler allows you to see through it, and a metal ruler is used as a straightedge when cutting templates and is the most accurate type.

Quiltmaking Techniques

Estimating amount of fabric: The directions for quilts shown here include approximate yardage for 45-inch-wide fabric. However, to determine your bed size, measure it fully made. This is, with bed pad, sheets, and blankets over the mattress. Measure the length, width, and depth including box spring. Decide if you want a slight overhang, an overhang with dust ruffle, or a drop to the floor, and whether the quilt will extend up and over the pillows.

To figure exact yardage, make a diagram on grid paper. One grid block represents 4 inches or 6 inches. Use this diagram as a guide when sewing together pieces for the final project.

Long ago, beds were shorter and squarer than the standard sizes as we know them. Some of the quilts shown here are wall hangings and are too square for today's bed sizes. However, where applicable to the design, we have included directions for altering the patterns to fit standard twin and queen- or double-size beds. If a design does not lend itself to any alteration in the pattern, we have given the size of the quilt shown and recommended a suggested bed size. Often a quilt can be altered in size by adding extra inches to the borders or by making them narrower.

Backing: The backing is the bottom layer of the quilt and is usually made from a lightweight fabric such as cotton. Unbleached muslin is a good material to use for this because it comes 60 inches wide and is quite inexpensive. Some of the quilts shown throughout the book specify the backing material if it will also be used as the quilt binding. In this case, the backing becomes a design element and will show on the front of the quilt as a border. Therefore you might want to select a color that matches or contrasts nicely with the colors used on the top of the quilt.

Once you've determined how much fabric you'll need for the backing, it will probably have to be pieced to cover the area. It is best to avoid running a seam down the center of the quilt backing. Cut 3 panels of fabric, and join 2 matching panels to each long side edge of a center panel. Press seams open.

Filler: The filler is usually called quilt batting or fiber fill and is a layer of fibers used between the quilt top and backing. This gives the quilt bulk and warmth but is lightweight and airy. You can buy this by the yard in most fabric stores.

If possible, cut batt to same size as quilt top. If the batting must be pieced, separate the layers where the 2 pieces will be joined. Cut a ½-inch strip from one layer and a similar strip from the adjoining edge. In this way when you sew the edges together you won't have a bulky seam.

Enlarging designs: Almost every design for quilting and pattern pieces in the book is shown same size. The letters for the Alphabet Quilt on pages 163–165, however, must be enlarged, as they will not fit same size on a page. In this case the designs are shown on a grid for easy enlargement.

If each square on the grid equals 1 inch, it means you will transfer or copy the design onto graph paper marked with 1-inch squares. Pads or sheets of graph paper are available in art-supply and needlework stores. Or, the back of self-adhesive paper, such as Con-Tact, is divided into 1-inch squares that are easy to use because the lines are boldly marked. If you don't have access to either of these, it's easy to rule off a sheet of paper in 1-inch squares.

Begin by counting the horizontal and vertical rows of squares on the design in the book. Count the same number of rows on your larger graph. Copy the design onto your grid one square at a time.

Patterns: The patterns for each quilt are shown full size. In this way no enlarging is required. Simply trace the design elements and transfer to template material (see below).

Making a template: Transfer the pattern to the template material by first tracing the design. Place this facedown on the cardboard and rub over each traced line. The outline will come off on the cardboard. For a sharper image, place a piece of carbon paper on the cardboard with the tracing on top. Go over each line with a pencil. Remove the tracing and cut out the design outline from the cardboard. Use sharp scissors or a craft knife.

Determine which fabric will be used for each template. Figure out the best layout for getting the most pieces from your fabric. For example, place all triangles on the fabric so they form squares. Mark around each template on the fabric. Since this will be your sewing line, each piece must be cut ¼ inch larger all around. If you're using a cotton blend rather than 100% cotton fabric, you might want to add ⅜-inch seam allowance. Cotton will turn and hold the crease, but the polyblend, for example, tends to spring back. Cut a piece to try it before cutting all pattern pieces.

Place each template ½ inch apart to allow for this extra fabric. Consider the grain of the fabric when placing your templates. As many long lines as possible should be on the grain.

Piecing: Although it is not faster, it is often easier to sew by hand. You can take your work with you or sew while relaxing. Also, some complicated designs are easier to do by hand. Since traditionally quilts were hand sewn, this is the preferred method of most purists. However, if you machine stitch, the work will go faster and be stronger than handwork.

Use a needle of recommended size (see page 16) and sew with small running stitches. Take 8 to 10 stitches per inch.

Sewing points: Many traditional quilt patterns are created from triangles, diamonds, and similar shapes. The points present a challenge and require special care.

When stitching 2 such pieces together, sew along the stitch line but do not sew into the seam allowance at each point. It helps to mark the finished points with a pin so you can begin and end your seams at these marks.

Sewing curves: With right sides facing, pin pieces together at spaced intervals around curved seam. Machine stitch with small stitches along seam line of convex side. Clip around almost to the seam line. When stitching the concave piece, start at the center and stitch to each outer edge. The convex piece should be on the bottom.

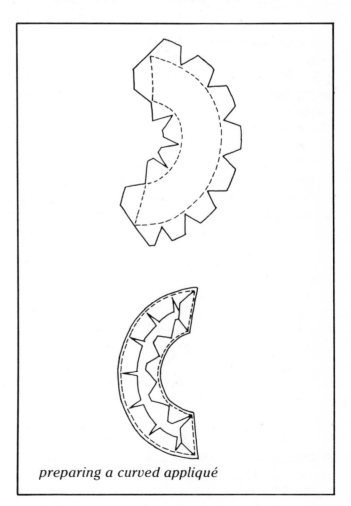

preparing a curved appliqué

Cutting blocks: When you add appliqué to the background fabric to create your blocks, the stitching causes the fabric to shrink in size. Therefore, when cutting out blocks, add an extra ½ inch all around. When the blocks are finished, you can remeasure them and trim to the size called for in the pattern.

Appliqué: When applying one fabric to another, you can use a matching thread or a contrasting one to define the appliquéd shapes. Pin or baste the shapes in place on the block. You can use an invisible hemming stitch or overcast the raw edges with embroidery floss. If you pin a small section, sew, and then repin another section, the appliqué will be smooth when finished. Check the back to be sure it isn't bunching as you sew.

Machine appliqué: Mark fabric with the template. When cutting, leave a ½-inch seam allowance. Pin the appliqué piece to the right side of the background fabric and stitch around the marked stitch line. Cut away the excess fabric as close to the stitch line as possible.

Use a narrow, short zigzag stitch all around the appliqué, covering the straight stitching line.

When appliquéing a pointed piece, such as the Turkey Tracks (see page 126), narrow the zigzag just before reaching the point on each side.

Sewing circles: Use your template to mark your sewing line. Cut fabric ¼ inch larger. Turn the extra fabric over the template and press all around, creating a crease. It may be necessary to clip around so it folds smoothly. Position the circular piece on the block and pin or baste.

Another method is to machine stitch around the fabric between the cut and stitch line. This makes it easier to turn the seam allowance all around, but takes longer.

Joining blocks: Once you have decided how you will quilt the top and this is done, you will set the quilt. With edges matching, place right sides of blocks to be joined on top of one another. Sew along bottom edge, leaving ¼-inch seam allowance. Continue to join blocks to create a row. When all rows are complete, join rows in the same way. Each seam must match up.

Borders: The border around the quilt binds the edges and can be done in one of two ways, depending on how you will finish the corners. Refer to the directions for finishing corners that follow before cutting your strips.

Cut your border strips with several inches added to the length for sewing shrinkage. The width of a strip should be cut with added seam allowance.

Place the front of one raw edge of the top or bottom strip on the quilt edge. Be sure that extra fabric is equal on both ends. Stitch according to directions for the kind of finished corners desired. Repeat on side strips to complete the border.

Finishing corners: Borders can overlap at the corners or the corners can be mitered. For overlapping, pin the long strips to the sides of the quilt with right sides together. Machine stitch, leaving a ¼-inch seam allowance. Repeat with the top and bottom strips. The hem on one edge of the quilt will be doubled over with the other edge on top of it. If you want to add a square of appliqué to each corner, do so with a matching piece from the overall design.

For mitered corners, pin the long border strips to the quilt with right sides together. These strips should extend a little more than the width of the adjoining border. Machine stitch, leaving a ¼-inch allowance. Repeat with the top and bottom strips, but do not pin to the lengthwise strips.

Stitch along one short edge. With face down on the quilt top, fold the extended piece up at a 45-degree angle. Press along the fold line. Fold the border down so the top side is up, and stitch the diagonal fold in place. Repeat at each corner.

For a double miter, fold the border strips in half lengthwise and press to form a crease. Press under ¼ inch on each raw edge for seam allowance.

Baste batting to the inside back of the strips. Attach edges and leave overlapping corners free. Trim excess fabric and batting of top and bottom strips so they are even with the outside edge of the long side strips.

Open the side strip and fold it over the cross strip. Trim excess fabric and batting to within 1 inch of the outside edge of the top and bottom strips. Fold the raw edge of the long strip under so it's even with the side strip. Pin corner edges together and turn front edge under at a 45-degree angle. Press and trim away excess fabric before stitching closed with a whipstitch.

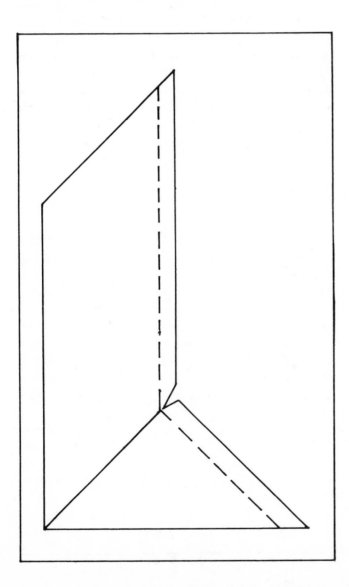

Joining blocks with strips: Each block is framed with a strip called a sash. Cut each strip the length of a block plus seam allowance. Pin right sides of one sash edge to one block edge and stitch together. Stitch blocks together to form rows.

Cut long strips for the vertical sashes. Pin right sides of one long edge to raw edge of a row of blocks and stitch together. Join all rows in this way. Be sure to have all seams and blocks lined up perfectly.

Self-finished edge: When adding the batting, do not let any batts from the strips overlap if you are quilting as you go (see page 24). Cut a piece of batting same size as the quilt top. Cut backing material 2 inches larger all around than the top. Baste all 3 layers together.

The backing is used to bind the edges. It is brought forward over the top. Turn the raw edge under ¼ inch and slip-stitch it to the quilt top. The corners are then mitered or overlapped (see pages 20–21).

Slip-stitch edges: Be sure that the batting does not interfere, then fold each raw edge of the backing and top to the inside ¼ inch (seam allowance) and slip-stitch together.

When using this method for finishing the edges, no extra fabric is needed. However, be sure that when you do your quilting, the stitches stop short of the seam allowance to allow for folding the fabric under.

Bias binding: Sometimes a quilt has a contrasting or matching piece of fabric that runs around the edges and rounds each corner (rather than a squared-off corner). To bind the edges with one continuous strip of fabric, you will have to use ready-made bias tape. Or you can make the strip from your quilt fabric. This is quite easy to do.

Plan this from the start so that you have enough fabric to cut all your quilt pieces and still have enough material to bind the edges.

1. To make one continuous bias strip, use a large piece of fabric (such as 1 yard) and mark the center of the width on both sides. Fold the fabric

in half diagonally and cut on this line (see diagram A).

2. With right sides together stitch both triangles along marked edges.

3. Mark parallel lines across the longest length at 4-inch intervals. (The finished edge of the quilt will be 1 inch.)

4. Seam the two opposite sides of the fabric together so that one edge is above the other by one 4-inch width. All other lines should match.

5. Cut around along the marked lines to create one long bias strip. Open seams and press.

6. Attach binding (see page 20).

Almost all of the trims on a quilt are ½ to 1 inch wide. Cut strips of fabric along the bias of the fabric. Each strip should be 4 times wider than your finished edge will be. In other words, for a ½-inch trim you will cut 2-inch-wide strips.

With right sides together and short edges aligned (each corner will not match), stitch together. Open seams and press. For cutting a continuous bias, see page 65.

Applying binding: With wrong sides facing, fold the bias strip in half lengthwise. If you're using cotton, you can finger-press on the fold and it will retain a crease. If you're using a cotton blend, it tends to spring back and will require pressing with a warm iron.

Open the strip and fold each edge toward the center crease and press. Open the top folded edge and pin facedown on the top of the quilt edge. Machine stitch along the fold line on the binding.

Turn remaining binding over raw edge to the back of the quilt. Pin the fold along the stitching on the back and slip-stitch in place.

Binding corners: If you are not overlapping or mitering corners, you will be binding them with the bias strip as you go around the quilt (see above). As you approach the corner, pin the binding to the quilt as you have done on the straight edge. Ease the fabric around the corner. Because it is cut on the bias, it will stretch to fit. Continue to pin and stitch the entire band all around.

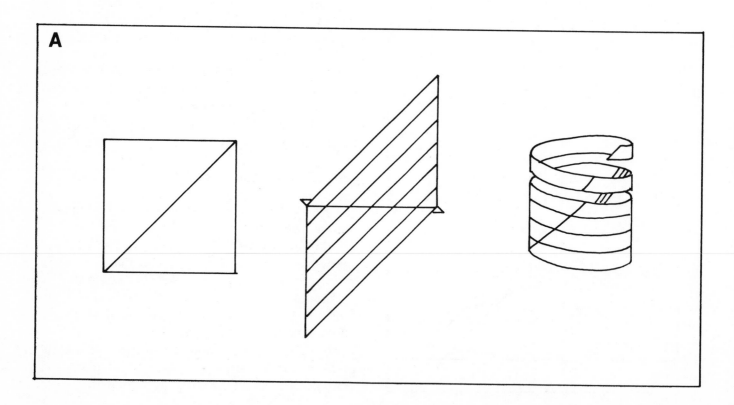

A

Quilting: Quilting is the means by which you will sew layers of fabric and batting together. The stitching can be done by hand or on your machine. These stitches define a design, making it appear almost three-dimensional and giving it a sculptured effect. The quilting is what makes a quilt interesting and gives it a textured look.

Hand quilting The most comfortable way to do your quilting is over a frame or in a hoop. The fabric remains taut, allowing you to make even stitches. It is important to have your fabric and batting basted and marked before quilting each section. When removed from the frame or hoop, your quilting will have a nicely puffed effect.

Keep your thread fairly short and take small, running stitches. Pull the knotted end through the backing fabric into the batting. Follow your pre-marked quilting pattern.

Machine quilting This is an easier, quicker method of quilting and creates a much different effect. It is best to do it when the batting isn't too thick.

Tufting This is often called "tying." Embroidery thread or crochet cotton is used to tie all three layers together at regular intervals. If the quilt is made of blocks, all four corners are tied as well as the center of each.

Using a single or double strand, start at the center of the quilt and work to the outer edges. Make one stitch through all layers, leaving a looped end. There should be less than ¼ inch between the points of entry. Cut and tie ends in a square knot, leaving the desired length. The tufts can show as a decorative element on the front of the quilt or tie on the back.

Basting: Before quilting, you will baste the quilt top, batting, and backing together. To avoid a lump of filler at any point, begin at the center of the top and baste with long, loose stitches outward, creating a sunburst pattern. There should be about 6 inches between the basted lines at the edges of the quilt. Baste from the top only. These stitches will be cut away as you do your quilting.

Outlining: This is the method of quilting just outside the lines of your appliquéd designs or along the patchwork seams. In this way, each design element is pronounced and the quilt is made secure. If you have many small patchwork pieces, you can stitch parallel lines across the designs. Plan these at regularly spaced intervals.

Overall quilting: When you want to fill large areas of the background with quilting, choose a simple design. The background quilting should not interfere with the patchwork or appliqué elements.

There are several popular patterns used for background quilting. These include a feather, interlocking circles, shell or scallops, and grid. You can easily create circles or scallops to the size desired by using a compass. Make grid patterns of squares or diamond shapes with a yardstick or masking tape for accurate spacing.

Border quilting: Often the border is decorated with its own quilting motif. This is usually a repeat pattern. Sometimes, if appropriate, the motif of the overall quilt is repeated around the border.

Marking patterns: Before basting the top, batting, and back together, you will mark the quilting design on the top of the quilt fabric. Spread the top on a hard, flat surface to transfer your design.

A light pencil is one way to mark your pattern. Another is with a water-soluble pen. Once all the quilting is complete, the lines that are visible can be removed with a plant mister. For dark fabrics, use an artist's white grease pencil.

Use a template when possible to mark your patterns. When making interlocking circles, mark the template where the lines connect. A yardstick is also handy for marking diagonal lines. Mark on the fabric along both edges of the yardstick, then flip it over and continue to mark along the edge for perfectly spaced quilting lines to follow.

Quilt-as-you-go

This is the method by which you quilt in sections, such as blocks, and then assemble the quilted pieces. In this way you can carry your quilting with you and work on parts of it at a time. It is also the only easy way to machine quilt. Once each block is quilted, the borders can also be made separately and then joined, to form the finished project.

1. Cut the top and backing section the same size, with ¼ inch all around for seam allowance.

2. Cut the batting slightly smaller so it will not catch in the seams.

3. Transfer the quilting design or make the block with pieced fabric (according to the design instructions for the individual project). Baste the 3 layers together, stitching from the center outward.

4. Quilt the block by hand or machine, but do not allow the stitching to extend into the seam allowance. Remove basting stitches.

5. With right sides of blocks together, join top pieces only (not the backing).

6. With blocks facedown, turn edges of backing under ¼ inch and slip-stitch together with each adjoining block. Filler should not overlap. If it does, trim so it butts at the seam line before sewing backing.

America's Favorite Quilts

Rolling Stone

This quilt is a 9-patch pattern and is sometimes called Single Wedding Ring or Wheel. If you look closely, you will notice the names of several members of a family marked in the center of each square.

Traditionally this quilt was made of one color and white, but here the use of a solid and a print makes an attractive contrast on the white background. The finished quilt measures 88 x 100 inches. This will fit a double or queen-size bed. To adjust the pattern for a twin, make 3 blocks across and 3 blocks down.

Materials
2⅔ yards solid red fabric
2⅔ yards yellow print
4⅔ yards white fabric
batting material
fabric for backing (6 yards of 45-inch-wide fabric)

Directions

To make one block

The quilt is made up of 30 blocks. Each block is 11 x 11 inches. To make one block, trace each design element and transfer to heavy paper for templates (see pages 15 and 17).
1. Cut out all patch pieces according to the chart. Add ¼-inch seam allowance to all pieces. You might find it convenient to make stacks of all separate sizes and mark each pile with the corresponding number.
2. Piece 4 squares by stitching four #4 triangles to each side of a #5 square. Open seams and press flat as you go along.
3. Make up 4 squares by piecing a #2 and a #3 oblong piece in contrasting colors.
4. Follow #1 block diagram to piece 3 squares together to create strips. You now have 3 strips of 3 squares each.
5. Piece the 3 strips together with right sides facing and seams aligned. Open seams and press.

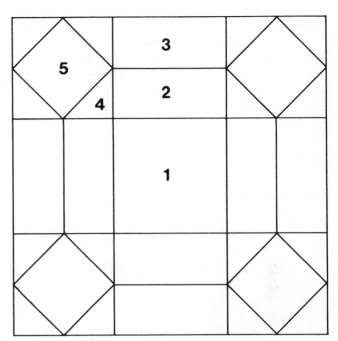

1. Block diagram

piece no.	in each block	in quilt
1	1	30
2	4	120
3	4	120
4	16	480
5	4	120
sashes		
6		46
7		71
border		
8		64
9		64
10		8

Joining blocks

To frame each block, you will be using 71 of the #7 strip with a #6 square at each block corner.
1. Join each pieced block with #7 strips between so you have 6 rows of 5 blocks each.
2. Piece six #6 squares to each short end of the remaining five #7 strips, making 7 sash strips.
3. With right sides facing and seams lined up, join all block rows to horizontal strips.

Making borders

For the inner border you will be using pieces #8, #9, and #10. You will also use four #6 squares for the corners.
1. With right sides together, piece each border strip. Open seams and press.
2. With right sides together at top and bottom edge, stitch border to joined blocks. Repeat on sides.
3. Cut 2 strips of white fabric 8½ x 104 inches for outer border (seam allowance is included). Cut 2 strips of white fabric 8½ x 75 inches. These strips have a few extra inches added to allow for shrinkage.
4. Attach border pieces (see page 20), and finish corners by overlapping (see pages 20–21).

Quilting

For various ways to quilt, see page 23.
1. Mark grid pattern on all white sashes. This can be done in the following way: Place a yardstick or metal straightedge diagonally across the top left-hand corner of the first sash and, using a pencil or water-soluble pen, draw the first line on the fabric. Turn the yardstick over without lifting it from the fabric and draw the next line. Continue to do this until all quilting lines have been precisely drawn.
2. Trace the quilting design for the outer border and transfer it to the fabric so that you have a continuous design that meets with a flower outline at each corner.
3. Trace and transfer each design to be placed in the center of each white #1 square on each block.
4. Cut batting to fit quilt top.
5. Cut backing material in half so you have 2

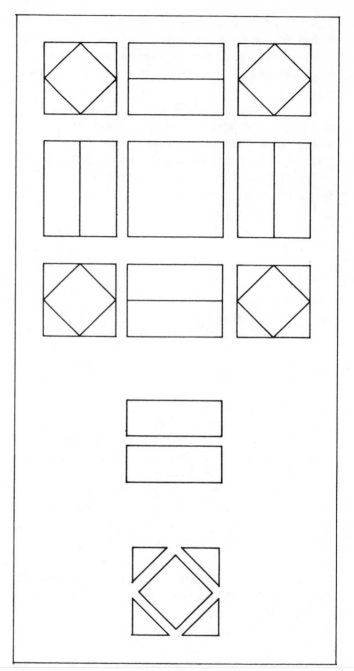

2. Block assembly diagram

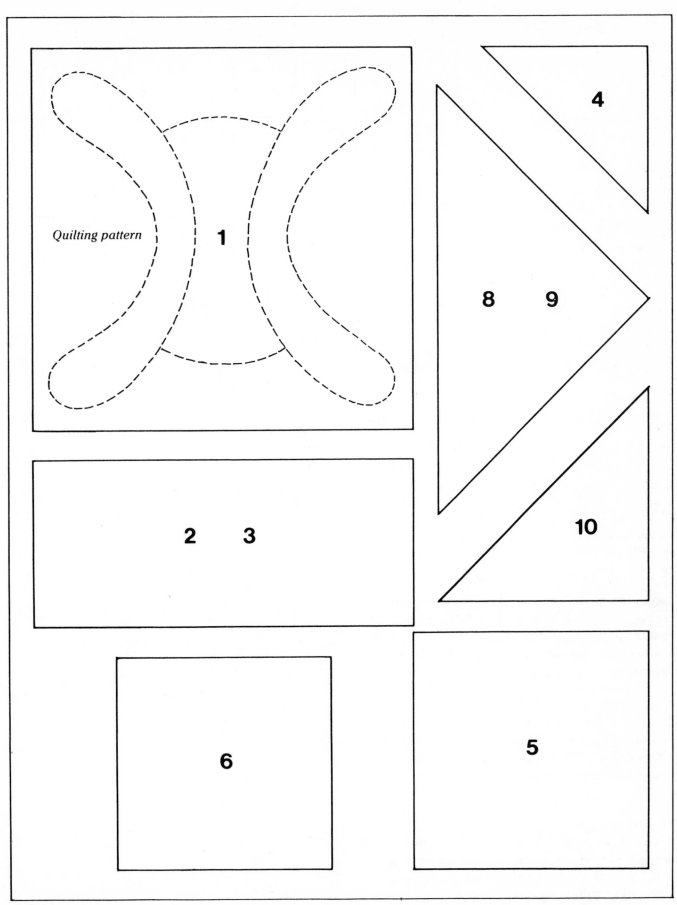

Quilting pattern

1

2   **3**

6

4

8   **9**

10

5

3. Pattern pieces

place on fold

7

3. Pattern pieces

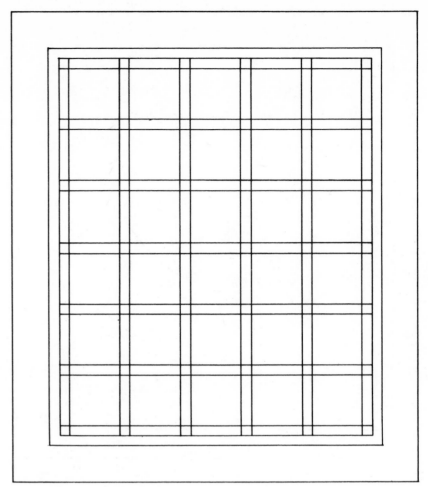

4. Quilt assembly diagram

pieces 45 x 108 inches. Seam them together to create one piece that is 90 x 108 inches. Press seams open.

6. Baste the backing to the top with the batting between.

To quilt: When quilting, use recommended quilting needles (see page 16) and take small, even stitches (about ⅛ inch apart) along the premarked quilting lines. Stitch along edges of both sides of patchwork pieces with matching or contrasting thread.

To finish

Trim backing to within 2 inches of quilt top all around. Turn raw edges forward ¼ inch and press. Fold down over the front of the quilt and blind-stitch to top, creating quilt binding.

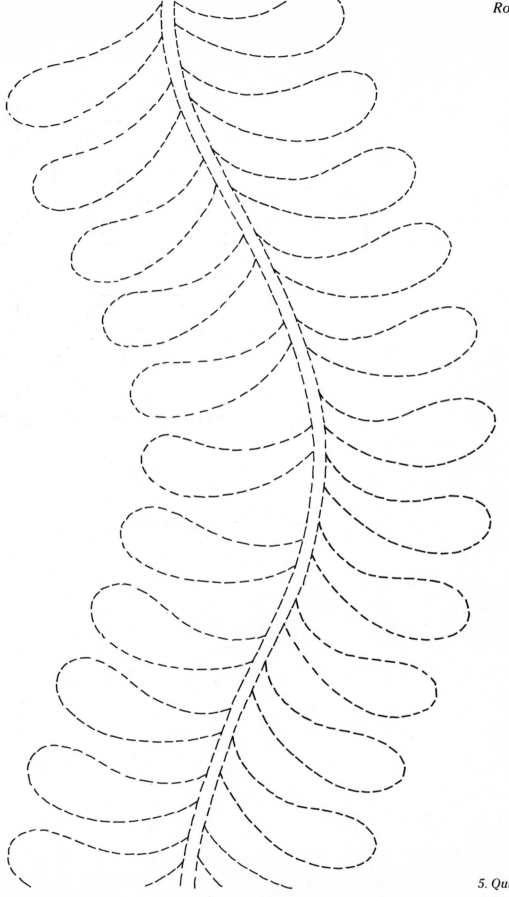

5. Quilting pattern

5. Quilting pattern

Le Moyne Star

This is one of the earliest star patterns, and variations of it that evolved can be seen in the Star of Bethlehem (page 100) and the Lone Star (page 169). Named for the founder of New Orleans, the Le Moyne Star became known in New England as the Lemon Star.

The quilt pictured here is made up of 2 colors, red and white. It makes a bold and dramatic statement, with the background and center of the stars in white and the star points and sashes in bright cherry red.

This quilt is 88 x 101 inches and will fit a queen-size bed. It requires 8 rows of 7 blocks. For a double bed you will need 8 rows of 6 blocks, and for a twin, 8 rows of 5 blocks.

Materials

7⅔ yards red fabric (backing included)
3 yards white fabric
batting material

Directions

To make one block

There are 56 blocks in the quilt. Each block is 10 x 10 inches. Refer to the chart to cut the number of pattern pieces required for each color.

1. Trace and transfer each pattern piece to heavy paper to cut a template (see pages 18–19). When cutting, remember to add ¼-inch seam allowance to each piece.
2. With right sides together and seams aligned, sew a red #2 to one side of a white #1 piece. Finger-press the seams open.
3. Next, join a #3 to the first #2 piece and then join this to the #1 piece. Refer to #1 block diagram and continue to piece star points #2 and #3 to the center piece #1. Open all seams and press.
4. With right sides together and seams aligned, join white triangle pieces #4 to the center points on each side of the star.
5. Piece white #5 squares to each corner to finish the block.

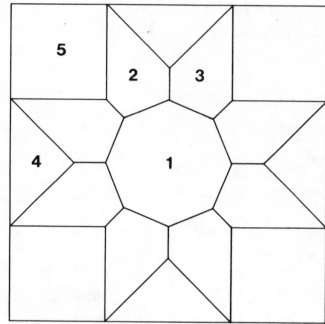

1. Block diagram

piece no.	in each block	in quilt
1	1	56
2	4	224
3	4	224
4	4	224
5	4	224

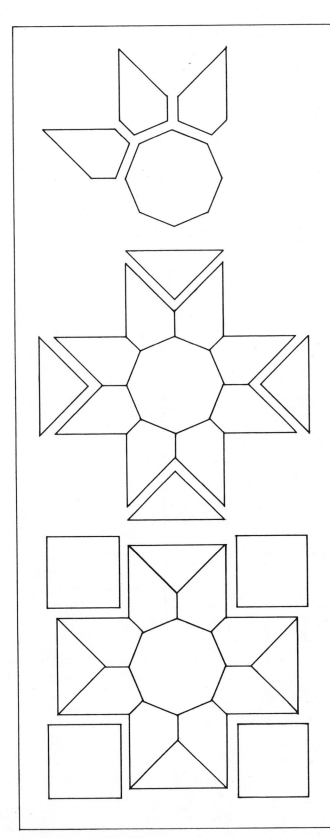

Making sashes

From the red fabric, cut 49 strips 3½ x 10½ inches and 6 strips 3½ x 101½ inches.

1. With right sides together, sew one 3½ x 10½–inch strip to the bottom edge of a block.
2. Continue to join sashes and blocks to create a row of 8 blocks. Open all seams and press.
3. Make 7 rows of 8 blocks each.

Joining rows

It is important to align all seams when adding the final sashes to join all rows of blocks.

1. Place the first long strip facedown on the first row of blocks. Stitch together. Open so all fabric is faceup.
2. Align the front edge of the long strip with the next row of blocks. This is where you will adjust the seams at top and bottom of each block. Stitch together. Continue to join all rows in this way.

Quilting

1. Trace the quilting design for the sashes and transfer to the 6 vertical sashes to make one continuous design.
2. Transfer the pattern to the center of each horizontal sash.
3. Cut batting same size as quilt top.
4. Cut backing from red fabric. You will have one panel 45 x 105 inches (this will allow for 4 extra inches on the length). Cut another panel 45 x 105 inches and then cut it in half lengthwise.
5. Join the 2 narrow panels to either long edge of the center panel, and press seams open.
6. Baste the top, batting, and backing together (see page 23).
7. Quilt with small running stitches along premarked pattern between blocks. Use red thread or white for contrast.
8. Next, quilt each block by running stitches along the inside and outside of each seam line. Quilt along seam line of sashes.

2. Block assembly diagram

4. Quilt assembly diagram

To finish

If you want to use the backing material to trim the edge of the quilt top, fold the raw edge from back to front ¼ inch and press. Fold ¼ inch again and stitch to front of quilt.

If bias tape is used to finish the edges, trim the backing to the same size as top. To make your own bias strip from fabric see pages 21–22.

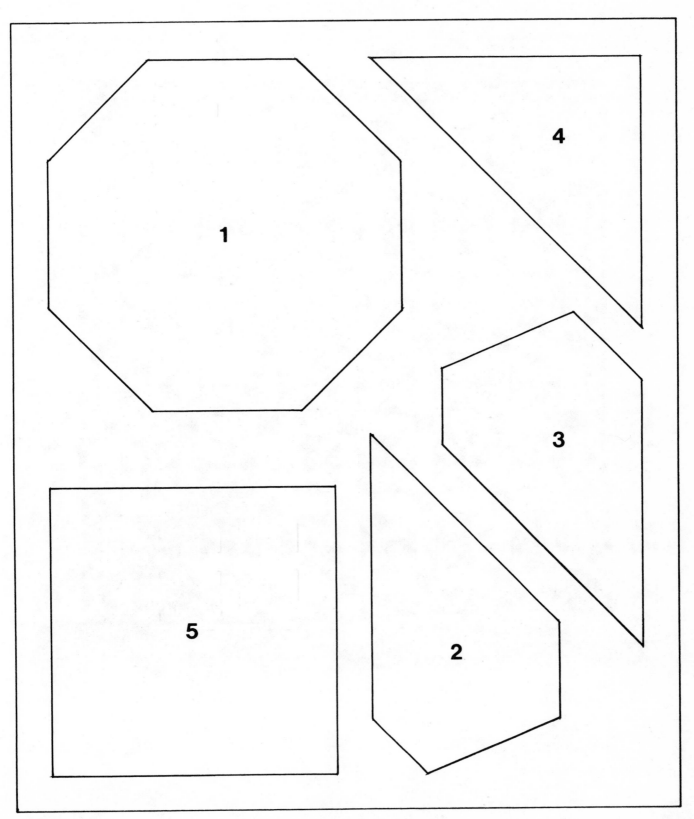

3. Pattern pieces

Railroad Crossing

Although worked here in 2 colors, red and white, this traditional American design would look good in a variety of color combinations. Done in different earth tones, it would give quite an interesting Indian feeling.

The quilting is difficult to see in the photograph, but each red triangle in the blocks is quilted in a heart shape. This design is repeated around the outside border as well.

The finished quilt is 89 x 89 inches, which will do for a queen or double bed, but the fit is better if you add another row of 6 blocks with 7 down. For a twin bed, make 4 blocks across and 7 down.

Materials
2⅔ yards red fabric
6 yards white fabric
batting and backing material

Directions

Trace and transfer the pattern pieces to heavy paper for cutting templates (see pages 15, 17, 18—19). Refer to the chart for number of pieces in each color. When cutting fabric, leave ¼-inch seam allowance.

To make one block
There are 36 blocks in the finished quilt. Each block is 8 x 8 inches.
1. Refer to #2 block assembly diagram for piecing sequence. Begin by piecing a #2 with a #3 on either side of it. Open seams and press.
2. Next, piece a #2, a #1, and a #2 together as shown.
3. Repeat step number one.
4. With right sides together and seams aligned, join the 3 sections to complete the block.

Joining blocks
Follow #3 pattern piece diagram to cut 84 strips of white fabric (piece #5) with ¼-inch seam allowance, and 49 red squares (piece #4).
1. Beginning at the left side of the first block, place one white strip facedown along the edge. Stitch together. Repeat on the right-hand side of the block.

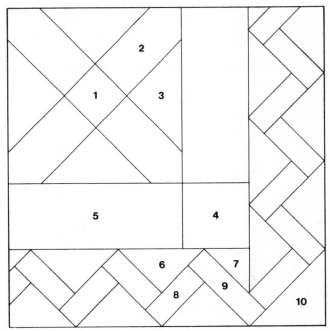

1. Block diagram

piece no.	in each block	in quilt
1	1	36
2	4	144
3	4	144
sashes		
4		49
5		84
border		
6		162
7		4
8		160

2. Continue to piece a row of blocks together with a sash between. Each row will have 6 joined blocks.

3. With right sides together and edges aligned, join a #4 piece to one short end of piece #5. Make 7 separate strips of sashes to horizontally divide each row of blocks.

4. Join rows of blocks with a long sash between.

Making borders

Refer to #1 block diagram to make inside borders. The quilt pictured here does not have a well-planned border. However, our pattern has been worked out so that the border should meet at the corners.

1. Cut all pieces according to the chart and join according to #1 diagram to make 2 strips 3½ x 70 inches and 2 more strips 3½ x 76 inches.

2. Join top and bottom border pieces first. Join side borders and finish with overlapping corners (see page 20).

3. Cut 2 strips of white fabric for the outside border 7½ x 89½ inches, and 2 strips 7½ x 69½ inches. Join at top and bottom and then sides with overlapping corners. If you prefer to miter the corners, see pages 20–21 for directions before cutting border fabric.

Quilting

Each red triangle in the blocks and each red square between sashes is quilted with a heart shape. There is no discernible pattern around the border, so you can create a grid or use one of the other quilt patterns. The scallop pattern on page 44 will fit around this border.

1. Transfer heart patterns to sashes as indicated in the diagram.

2. Transfer scallop pattern around the border.

3. Baste the top, batting, and backing together (see page 23).

4. For curved designs such as these (hearts and scallops), start quilting at the top of the curve and stitch in each direction from this point. In this way you are always quilting toward yourself, which makes it easier and the work more uniform.

5. Take small running stitches close together

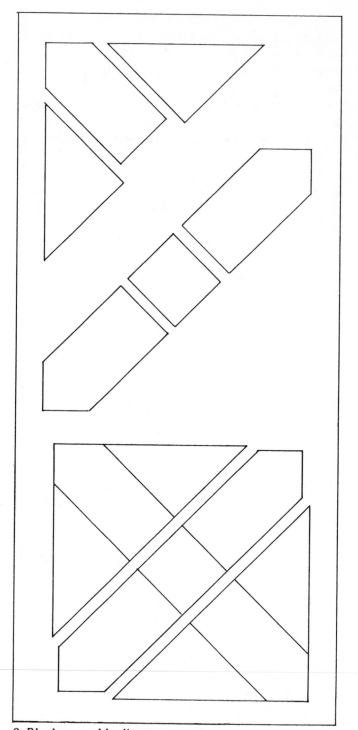

2. Block assembly diagram

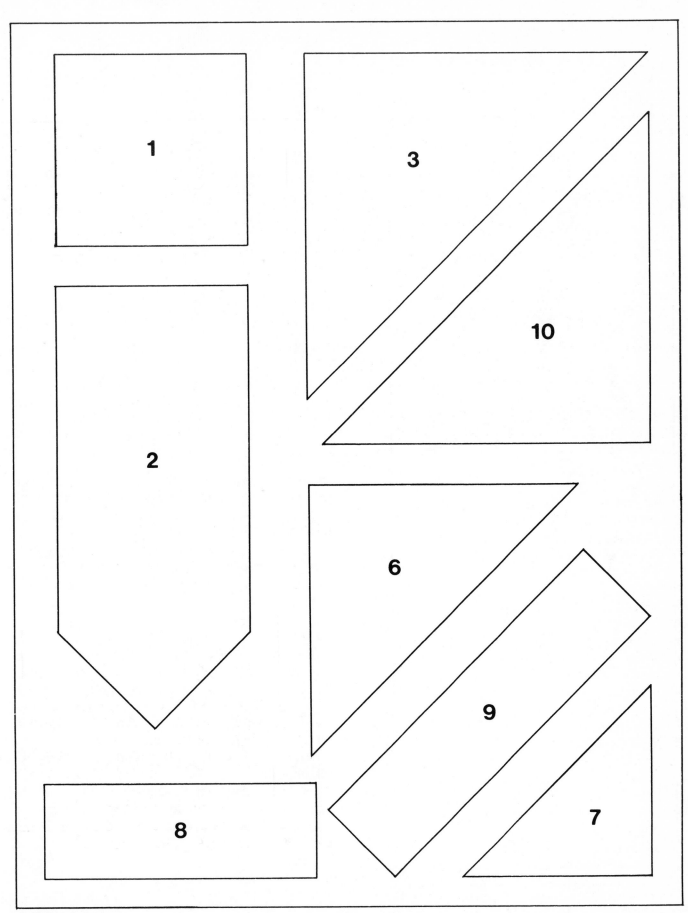

3. Pattern pieces

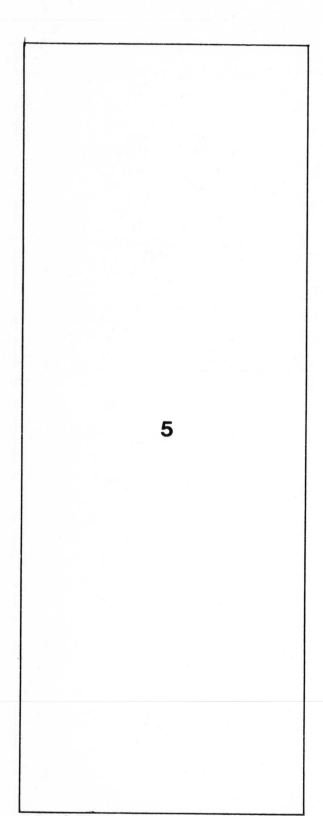

3. Pattern pieces

around the outline of each heart. If you want to do more quilting, consider following the seam line of each piece as well. If you use white thread, each heart shape will stand out.

6. Use white thread to quilt the border design. Be sure that the quilting stitches stop before the seam allowance so the edges can be turned under.

To finish

You can finish the edges of the quilt with bias tape, with fabric from the backing, or with a self-finishing edge. Most of the quilts have a 1- to 1½-inch edge made by bringing the backing fabric forward and stitching it to the top. The following directions are for self-finishing.

1. Trim away the filler if it extends to the edge of the material.

2. Fold the edge of the backing and top under ¼ inch and slip-stitch the folds together. If you want to add cording or a ruffle trim, simply insert the trim between the fabric, pin, and stitch all three together.

3. Press around outer edge of entire quilt.

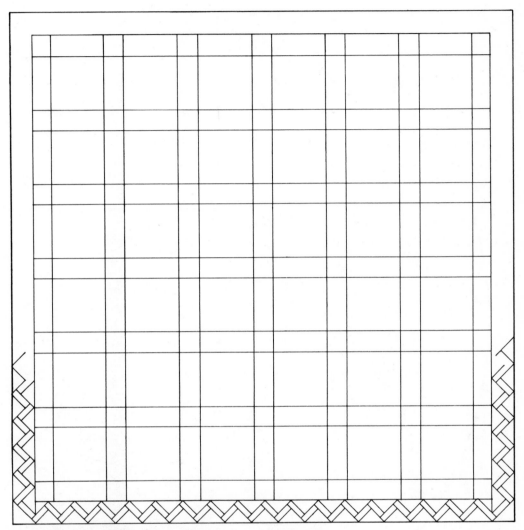

4. Quilt assembly diagram showing inside border detail. Outside border not shown.

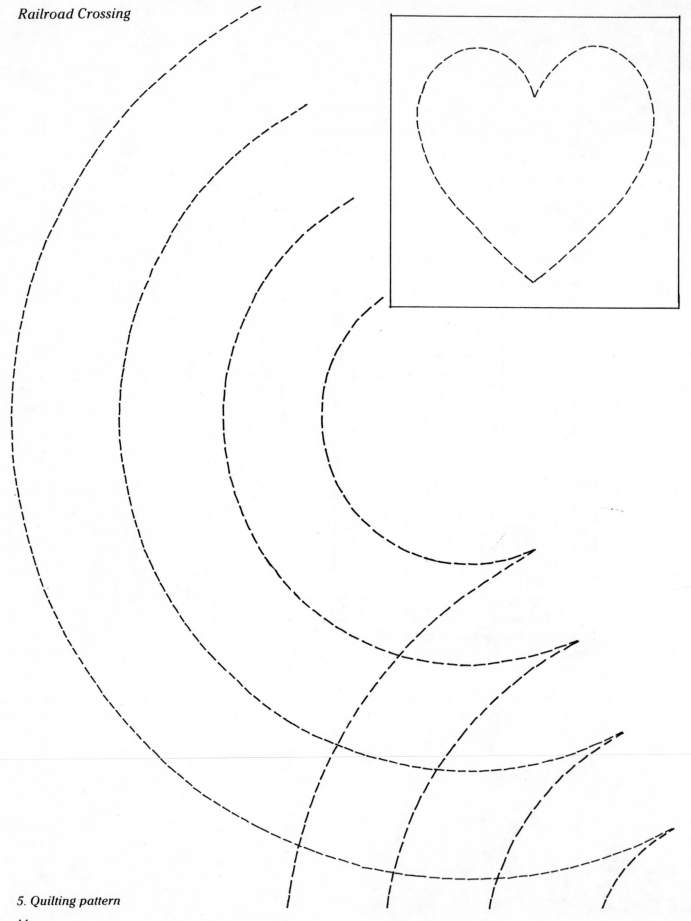

Railroad Crossing

5. Quilting pattern

44

This is another version of the Le Moyne Star seen on page 33. The combination of burnt-orange and dark brown is very attractive on a brown and white printed background. Accuracy of cutting and piecing is very important to make everything line up perfectly.

This quilt is 96 x 126 inches and will fit a double or queen- or king-size bed.

Materials
5 yards dark printed fabric
3 yards solid orange fabric
5 yards light printed fabric
batting and backing material

Directions

To make one block
The quilt is made up of 12 blocks. Each block is 24 x 24 inches square. Refer to #1 block diagram when piecing the blocks.

Begin by tracing each pattern piece and transferring to cardboard to make each template (see pages 18–19). When cutting from fabric, add ¼-inch seam allowance.

1. Piece the center star by joining a #1 and a #2 piece. Alternating dark (brown) and light (orange) diamond shapes, join all 8 points of the star.

2. Next join a #3 square (light print) between each star point. Open seams of the completed patch and press.

3. With right sides together and seams aligned, join a #1 and a #2 piece as indicated on the diagram. Piece this to one square piece #3.

4. Continue to join #1 and #2 pieces alternating light and dark fabric and join with each #3 until outer circle of diamonds has been formed.

5. Next add squares #3 where indicated between points.

6. Join #4 triangle pieces between remaining points. Open seams and press.

7. To finish block, join a #5 square to each corner.

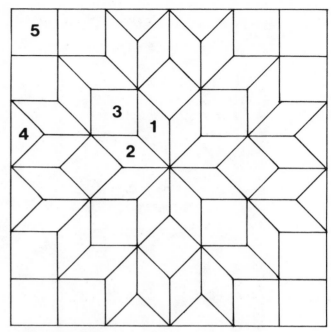

1. Block diagram

piece no.	in each block	in quilt
1	16	192
2	16	192
3	16	192
4	8	96
5	4	48
strips		
6		31
7		62
stars		
8		80
9		80
10		80
11		80

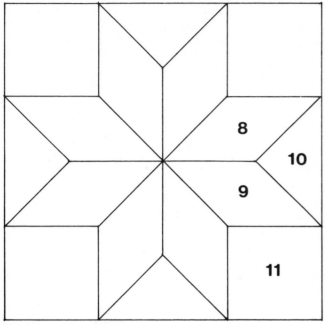

2. Corner star diagram

Joining blocks

You will now make 4 separate rows of 3 blocks each. Each block is framed by three 2-inch-wide sashes all around. Sash strips #6 and #7 are 2½ x 24½ inches.

1. With right sides together, piece a #7, a #6, and another #7 strip. Stitch to left side edge of the first block.

2. Add 3 strips in the same sequence to the opposite side of the block. Continue to join blocks in this manner.

3. Piece small star patch (diagram #2) as you did for the larger stars. Begin by piecing a #8 and a #9 piece together. Then join with a #11 square between the points at each corner.

4. Next, join a #8 to the #9 piece with a #10 triangle pieced between the points. Continue in this way alternating light and dark diamonds until the block is complete. Make 16.

5. Make horizontal sashes by piecing a #7, a #6, and a #7 strip together. Join a small star patch at each end of the 3 strips. Join 3 sections of strips with 4 small blocks. Make 5.

6. With right sides together, place top border strip across the top edge of the first row of 3 blocks. Stitch together.

3. Block assembly diagram

7. Repeat on lower edge of blocks and continue to join all rows in this way.

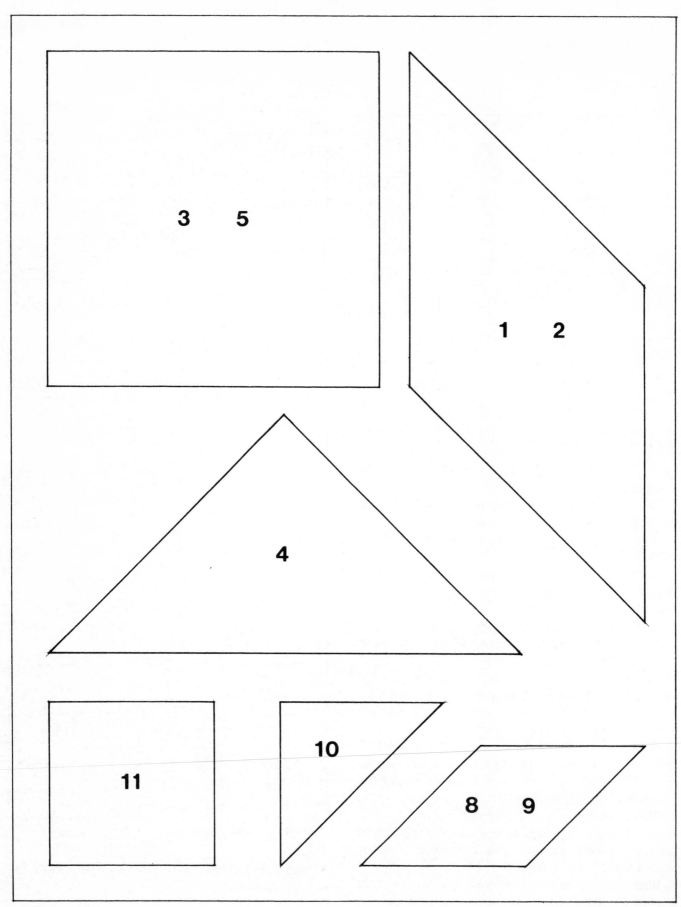

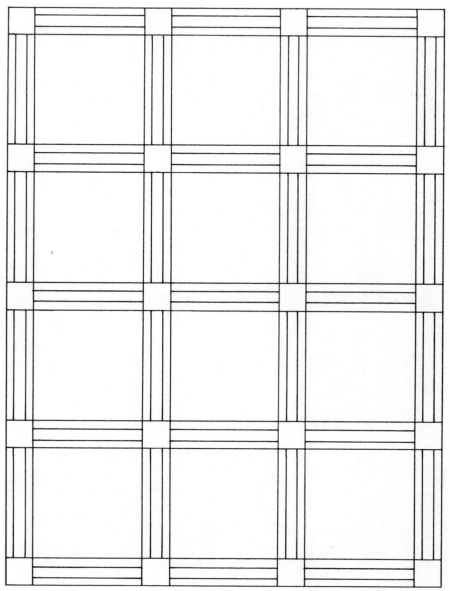

5. Quilt assembly diagram

Quilting

Cut batting and backing same size as top. Baste all 3 layers together with batting between. If the backing will be used to trim the edges, cut this piece at least 2 inches larger than the top.

There is no specific quilting pattern anywhere on this quilt. Simply follow all seam lines on the patches and stitch along both sides about ¼ inch from seam.

Little Red Schoolhouse

The house design has always been a popular quilt pattern. This one is quite striking because of its bold red, white, and green color combination and the regularity of the design. Because of the playful theme, it is often made with a variety of colorful prints. However the solids used here show a sophisticated use of this youthful design.

The finished quilt is 86 x 86 inches and makes a nice wall hanging. There are 25 blocks in all. For a better fit on a double or queen-size bed, make 5 blocks across and 6 down.

Materials
3 yards red fabric
2⅓ yards white fabric
3 yards green fabric
batting and backing material

Directions

Trace and transfer all pattern pieces to heavy paper to cut templates (see pages 18–19). The #15 and #16 are identical pieces only in reverse. If there is a right and wrong side of your white fabric, you will need two templates. Otherwise, you can cut all the pieces from one pattern and use them on one side or the other, as needed. When cutting fabric, add ¼-inch seam allowance. When piecing each block, refer to the sequence diagram as you go along.

To make one block
Each block is 12 x 12 inches. Make 25.
1. With right sides together, join a #1 piece to one long side of a #2 piece. Join a #1 piece to the opposite side of #2.
2. Next, join a #4 piece to the top edge of the 1-2-1 piece and a #3 piece to the bottom edge.
3. Place a #5 piece facedown on the larger pieced section along the right-hand edge as shown in block diagram. Open seams and press.
4. With right sides together and edges aligned, stitch a #7 piece to a #6 piece. Open seams and press. Join a #6 piece to the raw edge of a #7, followed by a #7 and a #6 piece. Open seams and press.

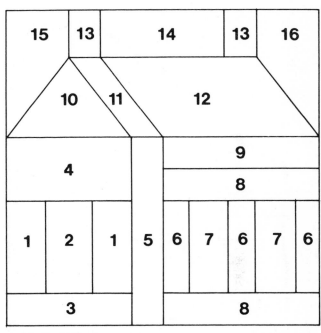

1. Block diagram

5. Join a #8 piece to the top edge of this pieced section. Add a #8 piece to the bottom edge.
6. Place a #9 piece facedown on the top #8 piece, with top edges aligned. Stitch across, open, and press seams.
7. Join a #10 to a #11 to a #12 piece. Open seams and press.
8. Next, join a #13, a #14, and a #13 together as shown.
9. Sew the 13-14-13 section to the top of the 10-11-12 section. Open seams and press.
10. Sew a #15 and a #16 piece to the outside edges of the #13 pieces, turning the corners at #10 and #12. When turning corners, clip in the seam allowance at the turning point before pressing seam open.

Joining pieces
You will now have 3 main sections of the block.
1. With right sides together and edges aligned, join section B with section C (on top) by stitching down the right-hand edge. Open and press.
2. Place section A facedown on the larger pieced section, with top edges aligned. Stitch across. Open and press.

51

piece no.	in each block	in quilt
1	2	50
2	1	25
3	1	25
4	1	25
5	1	25
6	3	75
7	2	50
8	2	50
9	1	25
10	1	25
11	1	25
12	1	25
13	2	50
14	1	25
15	1	25
16	1	25
sashes		
17 (red square)		16
18 (green strip)		40

Making sashes and joining blocks

The sashes between blocks are 4 x 12 inches. The red squares at each intersection are 4 x 4 inches. Cut 40 strips of green fabric 4½ x 12½ inches and 16 red squares 4½ x 4½ inches.

1. To join blocks, stitch a green sash #18 to the right-hand side of the first block.

2. Add the next block and continue to join blocks with sashes between. Make 5 separate rows of 5 blocks and 4 sashes.

3. To make horizontal sashes, place a red square #17 facedown on one short end of a green sash. Stitch together, open seams and press. Continue to join sashes with red squares between until you have 5 sashes joined by 4 red squares.

4. With right sides together and edges aligned, stitch a long sash to the bottom edge of the first row of blocks. Continue to join rows in this way. Open seams and press.

Making borders

The borders are made up of a narrow green strip, then a slightly wider red strip, with a wider green strip all around. The corners are mitered, and the edge is finished with white fabric backing.

1. Cut 4 strips of green fabric 1½ x 80 inches.

2. Cut 4 strips of red fabric 2 x 83 inches.

3. Cut 4 strips of green fabric 3 x 88 inches.

4. Join the inside borders first. There will be a little extra fabric at each corner, which will be trimmed when finishing corners. Do all 4 corners after all 3 borders have been joined to the top.

5. With right sides together, join red border to green.

6. Repeat with outside green border.

7. See pages 20–21 for mitering corners.

Quilting

Each pattern piece is marked with a quilting pattern that follows the line of the schoolhouse.

1. Trace the quilting lines and transfer to the fabric. Since the material is dark, use white chalk to mark the lines.

2. Mark the borders with diagonal lines evenly spaced. Using a yardstick, mark on either side, then flip it over. Continue to mark the quilt in this way.

3. For an overall diamond pattern, use the yardstick to mark across the quilt in the opposite direction as well.

4. Cut batting same size as top.

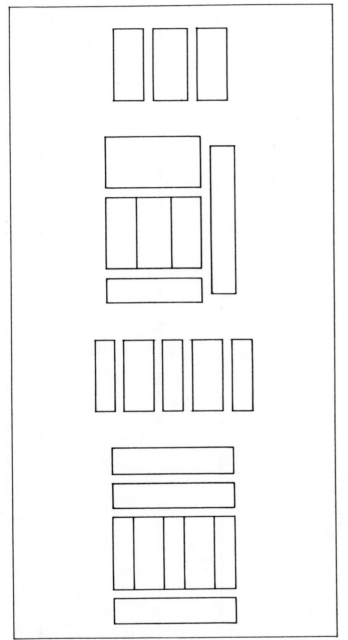

2. Block assembly diagram

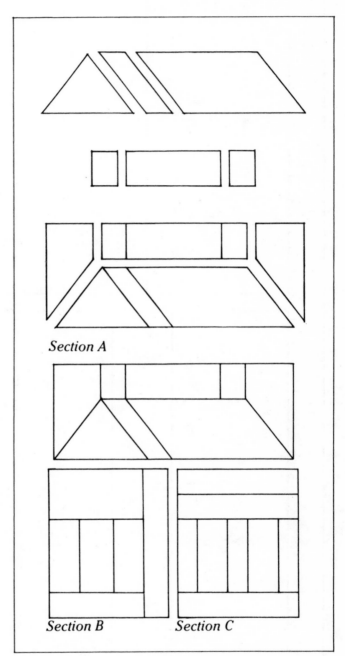

Section A

Section B   Section C

5. Cut white backing fabric 2 inches larger than the top. Baste all three layers together with batting between (see page 23).

6. Quilt along premarked lines, using white thread and taking tiny running stitches closely spaced.

To finish

Cut away basting thread. Turn seam allowance forward on backing and press. Turn the fabric forward over the quilt top and slip-stitch. The corners can overlap (see page 20).

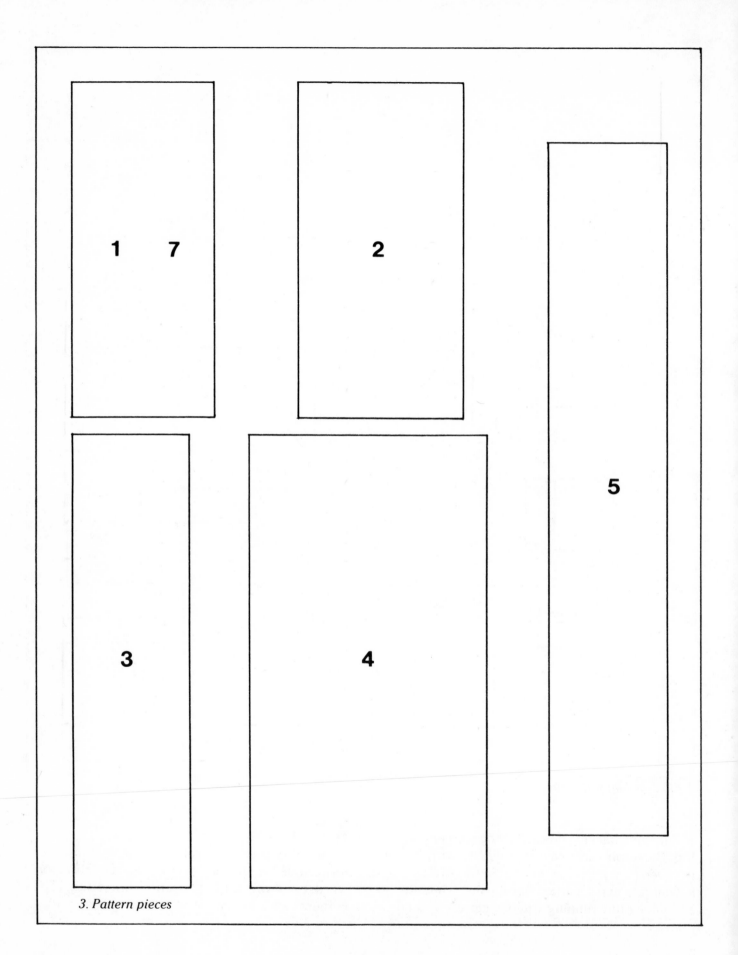

3. Pattern pieces

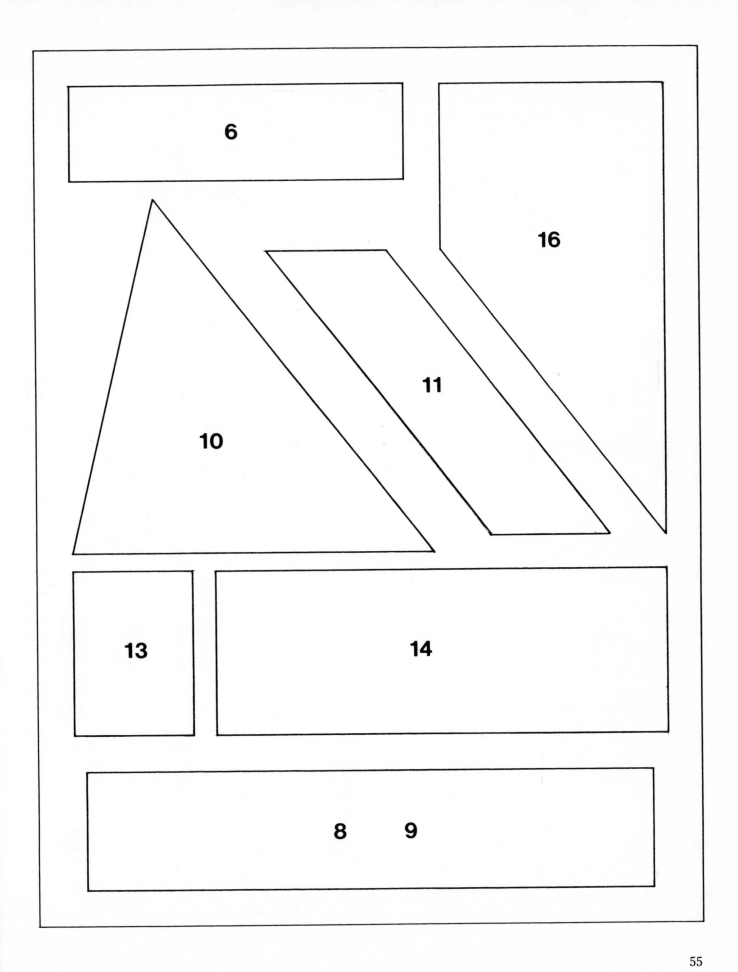

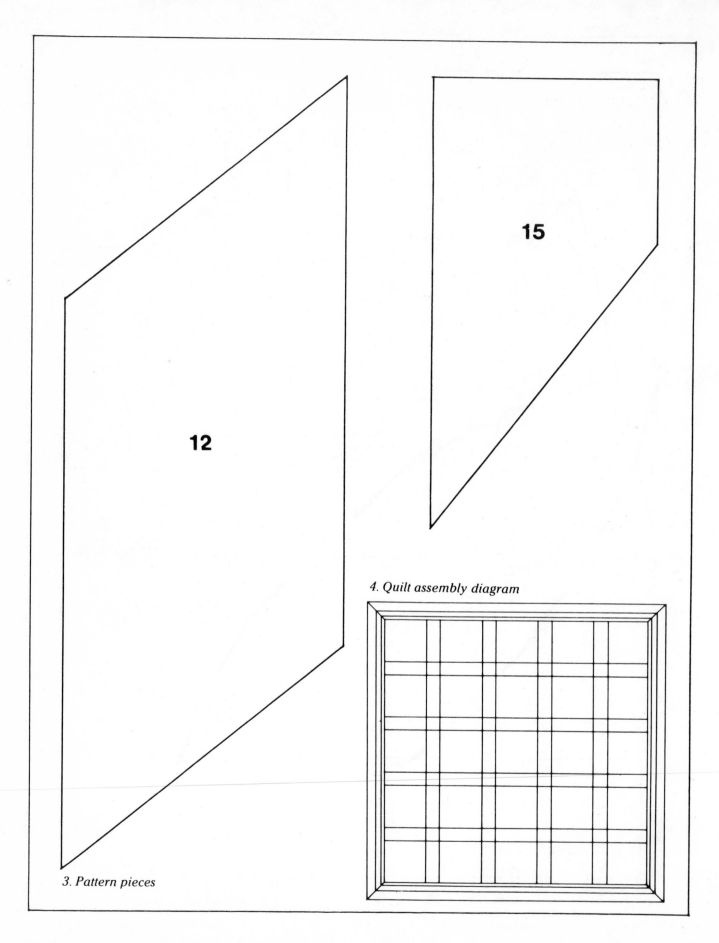

12

15

4. Quilt assembly diagram

3. Pattern pieces

Named for the Marquis de Lafayette, this lovely pattern is also known as simply Orange Peel or Melon Patch. It has been popular all over the United States and can be done in any color with white. The one pictured here is made with a red and green print with wide borders between blocks. Most often it is seen without sashes or borders.

This finished quilt is 64 x 64 inches, good for a wall hanging or as a lap throw. There are 4 rows of 4 blocks each. To make it for a twin-size bed, add 2 more rows of 4 blocks to extend the length.

Materials
3⅔ yards red printed fabric
2⅓ yards green printed fabric
2 yards white fabric
batting and backing material (white fabric used here)

Directions

To make one block

There are 16 blocks in this quilt. Each block is 11 x 11 inches when finished. Since there is a lot of piecing of curved sections, refer to page 19 in the techniques section before beginning.

Refer to #1 block diagram for piecing colors indicated. Trace and transfer pattern pieces to heavy paper to cut templates. When cutting each piece, add ¼-inch seam allowance.

1. Piece a #1 and a #3 piece together in the following way: Stay-stitch along one curved edge of #3. Clip the seam allowance to the stay-stitching line. With right sides together and clipped piece on top, align curved edges and stitch.

2. Clip and piece the opposite curved edge of the #3 piece with a #2 piece in the same way. Continue to do this until all pieces in the block are joined.

Joining blocks

Cut 12 strips 4½ x 11½ inches from the red printed fabric.

1. With right sides together, place a sash along the right side edge of the first block. Stitch together.

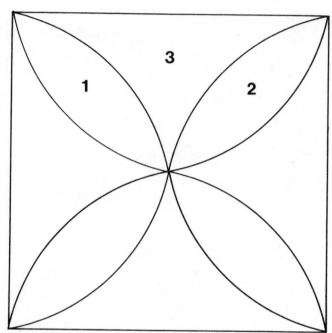

1. Block diagram

piece no.	in each block	in quilt
1	2	32
2	2	32
3	4	64
border		
4		60
5		60

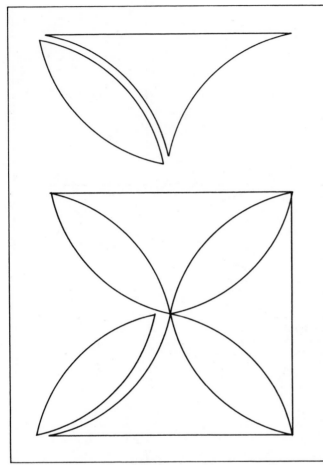

2. Block assembly diagram

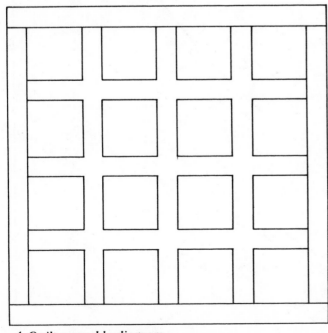

4. Quilt assembly diagram

Continue to add blocks across to make a row. Make 4 separate rows of 4 blocks.

2. Cut 3 strips 4½ x 56½ inches from red fabric.

3. Join all rows, making sure that blocks and seams are aligned.

Making borders

The border is pieced with alternating #4 and #5 triangles of the red and green printed fabric. Begin by cutting out the number of pieces required for each color. Follow the photograph for alternating colors and joining to create 4 border strips.

1. With right sides together and edges aligned, stitch sides to quilt top first. Open and press seams.

2. Join the top and bottom strips in the same way.

Quilting

The quilting on this quilt is a simple vertical pattern. The stitches create evenly spaced lines going in one direction across the blocks and sashes. The quilting lines go in the opposite direction on the outside border.

Some quilters prefer to quilt following the seam lines of each patch with a grid of stitches on the sashes. Either way is equally effective.

1. Begin by marking your quilting lines on the top of the quilt.

2. Cut backing material 2 inches larger than quilt top. Cut batting same size as top.

3. Baste top, batting, and backing together.

4. Take small running stitches along all premarked quilting lines or along all seam lines.

To finish

Turn raw edge of backing forward ¼ inch and press. Fold over to front of top, and blindstitch. There will be a narrow white trim all around the quilt.

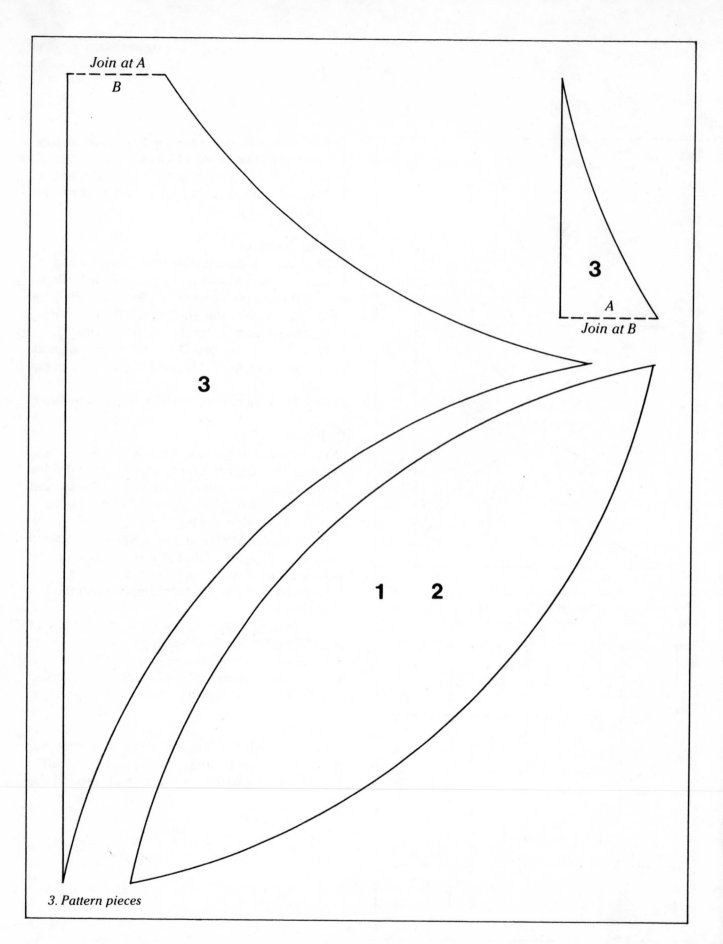

Join at A

B

3

A

Join at B

3

1 2

3. Pattern pieces

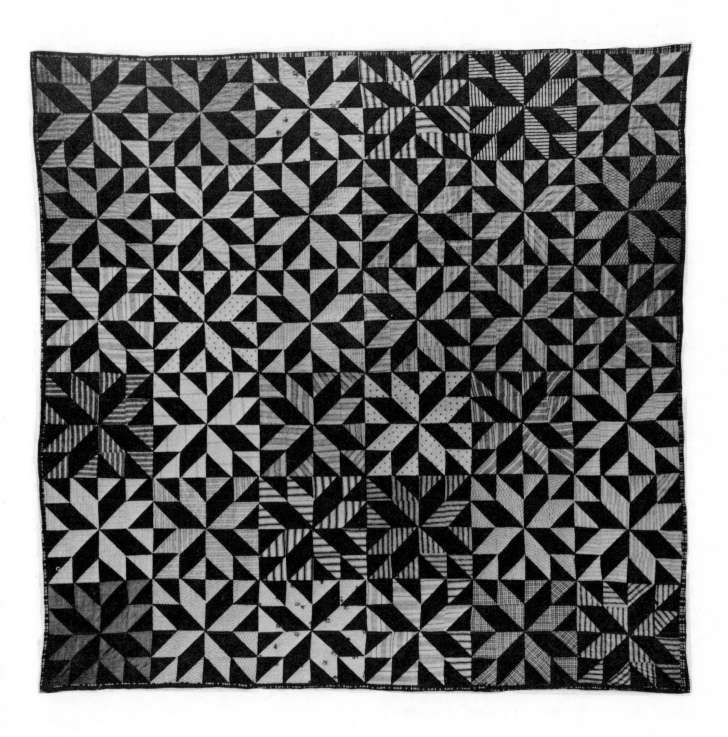

This version of the Le Moyne Star quilt is made from shirt fabric, and each block uses one pattern with a contrasting darker print. The shirt fabric is a light cotton print, mostly stripes in red, white, or blue colors.

If you are buying fabric rather than using left-over scraps, a striped ticking material in red and white or blue and white will be attractive.

This quilt is made up of 6 rows of 6 blocks, creating an overall size of 84 x 84 inches. This will fit a double-bed size as well as a queen-size without going up and over the pillows. If you add one more row of blocks to the bottom, the quilt will be 84 x 98 inches, which will be a better fit for a queen-size bed. For a twin, make 7 rows of 5 blocks, which will measure 70 x 98 inches.

Materials
4 yards dark printed fabric
4 yards light printed fabric
batting and backing material

Directions

To make one block

Each block is 14 x 14 inches, and there are 36 blocks in the quilt. The entire pattern can be made with 2 patches, the triangle and the diamond shape.

Begin by tracing and transferring the pattern pieces to cardboard to make templates (see pages 18–19). Refer to the chart for cutting the number of pieces from the light and dark fabrics. Remember to leave ¼-inch seam allowance when cutting out the fabric.

1. If you are making this quilt from one triangle piece (rather than triangles and diamonds), you can make each block in strips of 8 pieces each. To make it as shown, refer to #1 block diagram for color and piece sequence.

2. With right sides together and edges aligned, join a diamond piece #1 with the same shape #2 (light and dark fabric).

3. Next, join 2 triangles #3 and #4 to create a square. Piece together with #1 and #2.

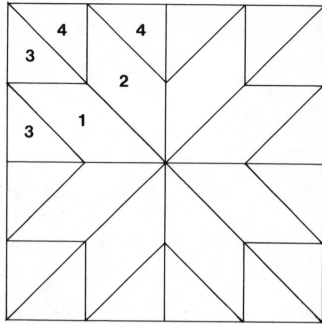

1. Block diagram

piece no.	in each block	in quilt
1	4	144
2	4	144
3	8	288
4	8	288

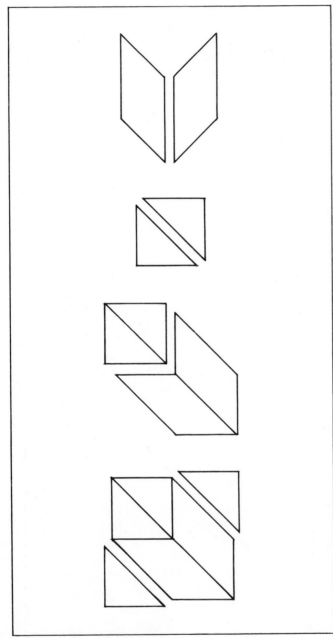

2. Block assembly diagram

4. Join a #3 and #4 as indicated to create a square section. Repeat steps 2 through 4 three more times to make 4 square sections of one block.
5. Piece all 4 sections together to make up one block.

Joining blocks

Refer to #2 block assembly diagram for joining blocks. As you can see, there are no sashes or borders in this quilt. It is important to align all seams when joining blocks.

Make separate horizontal rows and then join all rows by placing one row facedown on the first, with bottom edges even. When pinning, check to be sure individual patch seams are aligned correctly. Stitch across. Open seams and press. Repeat with each row of blocks.

Quilting

This quilt has an overall grid of 1-inch squares. However, you may prefer to stitch ¼ inch on either side of seam lines on each pieced patch. If using the grid pattern, mark quilting lines with a yardstick and soft pencil.
1. Cut batting and backing same size as top of quilt.

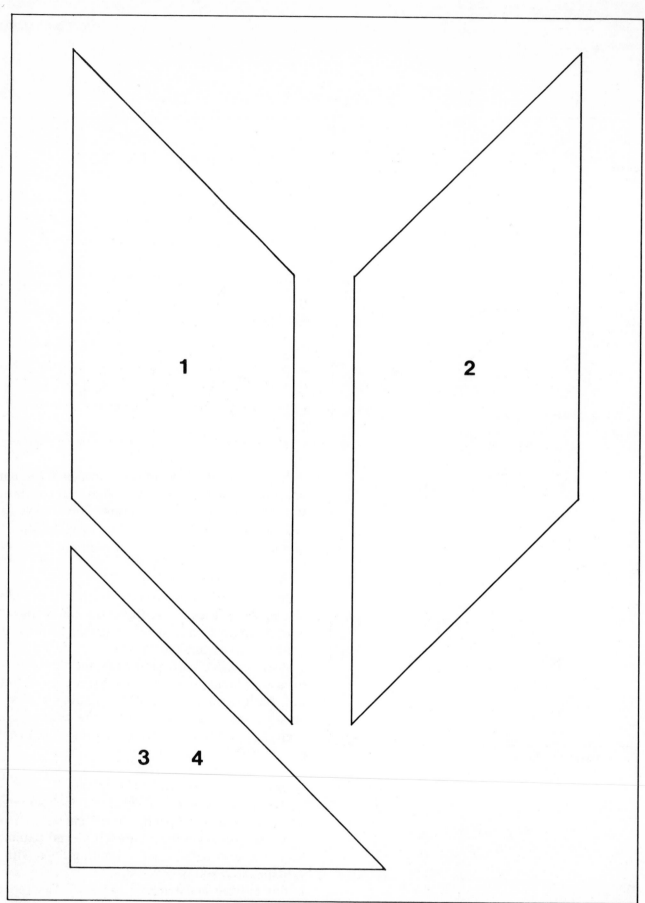

3. Pattern pieces

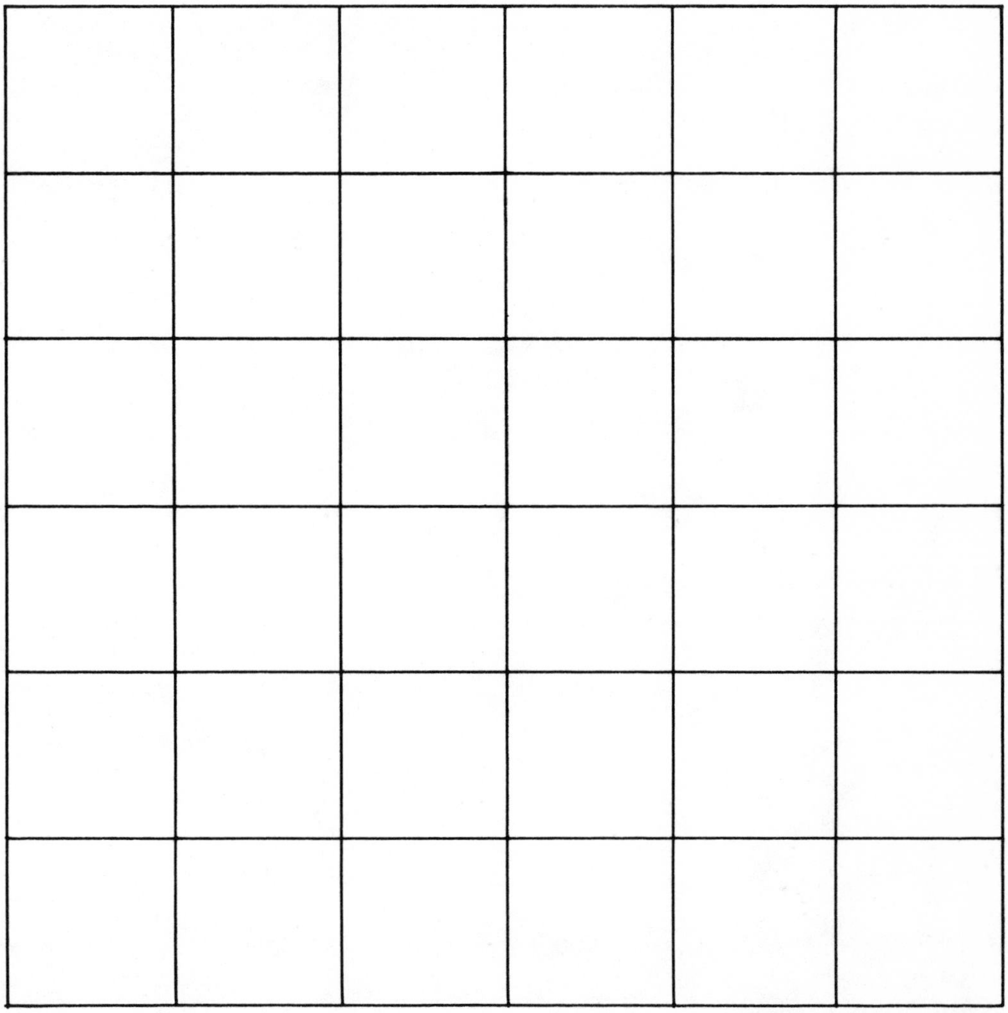

4. Quilt assembly diagram

2. Baste top, batting, and backing together (see page 23).
3. Begin at arm's length away from you and take small running stitches toward you to quilt.

To finish

The edge of this quilt is finished off with a bias strip of fabric not used in the patchwork pattern. However, you can choose any of the material from a block or use the dark printed fabric for the finish. This can also be used for the backing, if practical.

Teacup

This delightful design is perfect for using up all the scraps in your sewing basket. Perhaps that's how the original idea came about. Can't you imagine the quiltmaker of long ago sitting down to a cup of tea with her scraps of fabric spread before her? Household items were often used as inspiration for simple designs that were easy to draw and reproduce in fabric shapes. This is a perfect example of a repeat appliqué pattern.

The finished quilt size is 84 x 98 inches and fit for a queen-size bed. There are 9 blocks across and 10 down. For a twin, make 7 across and 10 down.

Materials
3⅓ yards white fabric
3 yards printed fabric for sashes
variety of scrap material for teacups and sash intersections
batting and backing material

Directions

Trace each pattern piece, and transfer to heavy paper for cutting a template (see pages 15, 17, 18–19). The teacup is made from 3 pieces that can be joined together and then appliquéd to the block. Or each piece can be applied separately. It is easier to center each appliqué if it is applied as a whole. Therefore, the following directions are for this method. Cut each teacup piece from the same fabric. As you can see from the photograph, some of the appliqués are cut from the same material but placed far enough apart so as to create an overall patchwork pattern. When cutting out each fabric piece, be sure to add ¼-inch seam allowance.

Preparing the appliqué
1. Stay-stitch around the curved edge of each side of the teacup handle (#2), ¼ inch from edge. Clip around inside curve to stitch line. Notch outside curve to stitch line. (See diagram A.)
2. Turn both edges under to wrong side along stitch line, and press. With right sides facing and notches matching, pin handle #2 in place on cup piece #1. Stitch across each end of handle. Press seams toward teacup.

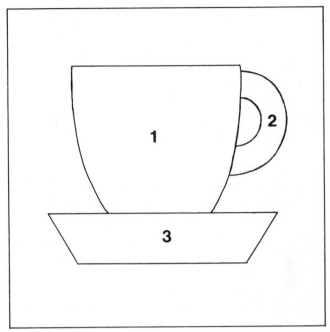

1. Block diagram

piece no.	in each block	in quilt
1	1	90
2	1	90
3	1	90
sashes		
4 (corners)		352
5 (strips)		179

67

3. Place piece #3 on piece #1, with notches matching. Stitch across between notches. Press seams down toward base of cup.

4. Turn all raw edges under along stitch line, and press. Make 90.

To make one block

1. Cut a square of white fabric 7½ x 7½ inches.

2. Draw a square 7½ x 7½ inches on tracing paper. Center the template on the paper and draw around it. Use this to center all appliqués on each block.

3. Place the tracing over the white fabric and slip the appliqué under the tracing where you have drawn the teacup. Remove the tracing and pin the appliqué to the fabric. The tracing will enable you to center each appliqué perfectly so that each block is symmetrical.

4. Blindstitch around the edge of the teacup. If you quilt each block as you go (rather than after the entire quilt has been assembled), hand-stitch along each edge of each piece, as with pieced quilts.

Joining blocks

1. Cut 179 strips of printed fabric 3 x 7½ inches for sashes (#5 pattern piece). Cut 176 squares (#4 pattern piece) of red fabric, and 176 squares from various scrap fabric patterns. Each of the squares separating the sashes is made up of 2 red and 2 printed squares.

2. With right sides together and side edges aligned, join a red square to a printed square. Repeat.

3. With right sides together, join all 4 squares so you have a print and a red together on top of a red and a print. Open seams and press. Make up 88 of this combination. Refer to color plate necessary.

4. Using a large flat surface, arrange all the blocks so you have 10 rows of 9 blocks each. Rearrange and move the blocks around until you have a pleasing combination of colors and prints with solids.

5. With right sides together and top edges aligned, place a sash strip on top of the first block. Sew

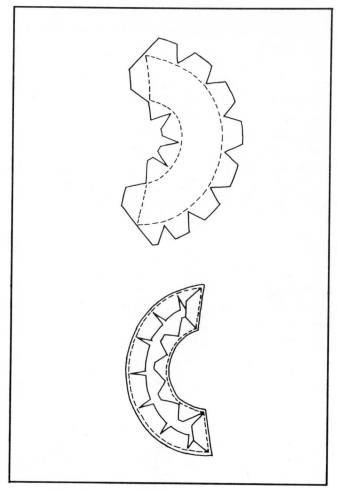

preparing a curved appliqué

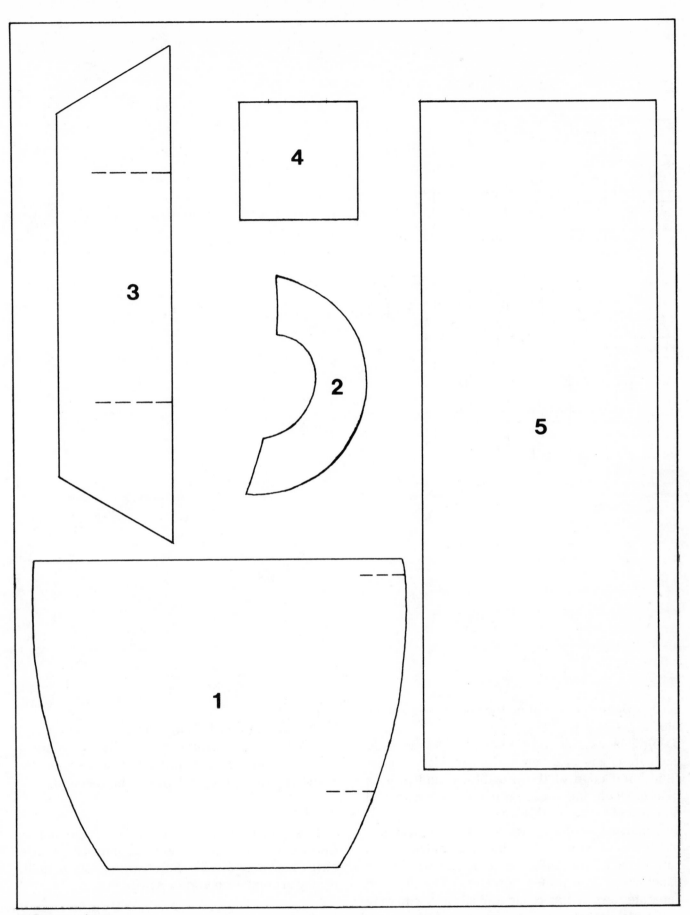

3. Pattern pieces

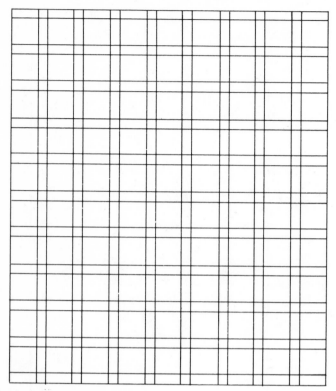

4. Quilt assembly diagram

across. Open and repeat on the bottom edge of the block.

6. Join a block of squares made up of #4 pieces to each short end of a new sash strip. Place on the right-hand edge of the first block, and join as before. Open and press seams. Continue to add blocks and sashes in this way.

Because the blocks are small, and there are many pieces to join, each block is added to the row above as you build the quilt. This will insure exactness. If you prefer, however, you can make separate rows of blocks and join all rows with long horizontal sashes.

Quilting

Cut batting and backing same size as top and baste all 3 layers together. Quilt with tiny running stitches around teacup and along sash seams. Do the same with each patch in the intersections.

To finish

This quilt is edged with a border of pink fabric. Choose any color from the quilt and make a bias strip (see pages 21–22). Stitch around entire quilt, easing around each corner as you go.

This is another version of the Le Moyne Star and provides a good use for scrap material. Each block combines light and dark fabrics in a different print. For a more uniform design, you might like to choose one dark and one light print to use throughout.

The alternate white blocks and the border are excellent examples of traditional quilting designs.

The finished quilt is 90 x 90 inches and will fit a queen-size or double bed. There are 16 pieced blocks, alternating with 9 white quilted blocks.

Materials
3 yards dark printed fabric
2 yards light printed fabric
5 yards white fabric
batting and backing material

Directions

To make one block
Each block is 14 x 14 inches, and there are 16 blocks made of the same pattern pieces. Refer to #1 block diagram when assembling the pieces.
1. Trace and transfer the pattern pieces to heavy paper for cutting templates (see page 17).
2. Refer to the chart for cutting the number of pieces in each fabric. Each block can be different, or you can use the same contrasting material in each block.
3. Begin by making the center star. With right sides facing, join two #1 pieces. Next, join a #1 on each side of the pieced patch. You will now have the top half (4 points) of the star.
4. Join four more #1 pieces in the same way. With right sides together join the two halves. Open and press seams open.
5. Join a #2 square between points all around.
6. Piece a #2 square between center points on each side.
7. Piece six #1 diamond shapes together as you did for the center star (eliminating 2 pieces). Make 4 such pieces.
8. Join each 6-pointed star to the center patch, as indicated on the diagram.

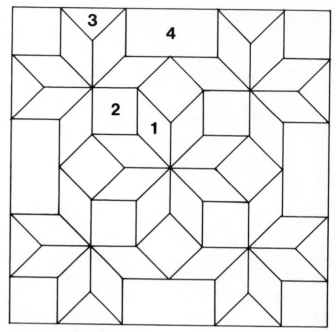

1. Block diagram

piece no.	in each block	in quilt
1	32	512
2	12	192
3	8	128
4	4	64

2. Block assembly diagram

9. Piece the #4 rectangle between stars to join them.

10. Join a #3 triangle where indicated, and piece a #2 between remaining points at each corner. This will complete the block.

Cutting the quilting blocks

As you can see, the blocks are joined on the diagonal, creating an overall diamond pattern. Each of the plain quilting blocks can be marked with the quilting pattern before they are joined with the patchwork blocks, or after they are assembled.

1. Cut 9 squares (A) of white fabric 14½ x 14½ inches.

2. To be sure that the 12 border triangles (B) are the exact size needed, draw a pattern of a 14½-inch square on paper. Cut this in half on the diagonal, from corner to corner. Pin this pattern piece to your white fabric, and when cutting out, add ¼ inch to the cut edge to allow for seaming. Cut 9.

3. Cut the triangle pattern in half to use for the 4 corner pieces (C) on the quilt top. Add ¼ inch to each cut side when cutting out the fabric.

Joining blocks

1. With right sides together and edges aligned, join corner triangle piece (C) with first block.

2. Join a border triangle (B) with one side of first block.

3. Join another border triangle (B) to the opposite side of first block, creating a larger triangle. Continue to make rows of blocks according to the diagram.

4. With right sides together, join the first section to the next row of blocks and triangles. Continue to do this until all rows are joined. End with a corner triangle (C).

Adding borders

Cut 2 strips of white fabric 5½ x 92 inches and 2 strips 5½ x 82 inches. The finished width of the borders is 5 inches, and we've added 2 inches to the length of each side that will be cut to size after they're joined. These are overlapping corners (see page 20).

Marking quilt pattern

The quilting pattern for the blocks and triangles (diagram #5) is perfect for the corner (C) triangles. For the blocks, do the following:

1. With a white block on the diagonal, find the center point. Trace and transfer the quilting design to the top quarter of the block.

2. Turn the pattern over and transfer it to the opposite top quarter. Repeat on the bottom to join the design.

3. Trace and transfer half of the pattern to each border triangle (B).

4. Trace and transfer border pattern to create one continuous design. Take special care on the corners.

5. Refer to diagram for grid pattern on white blocks.

6. Quilting pattern on pieced blocks is made up of evenly spaced parallel lines marked on the diagonal. If you prefer, you can stitch ¼ inch from either side of seam lines on each piece.

Quilting

Cut backing and batting material same size as top. Baste all 3 layers together (see page 23). Take small, close running stitches along premarked lines.

To finish

The edges are finished with a dark printed fabric made into a bias strip (see pages 21–22). If you want to use the backing material for the finished edge, be sure to cut the material 2 inches larger than the top (See page 36).

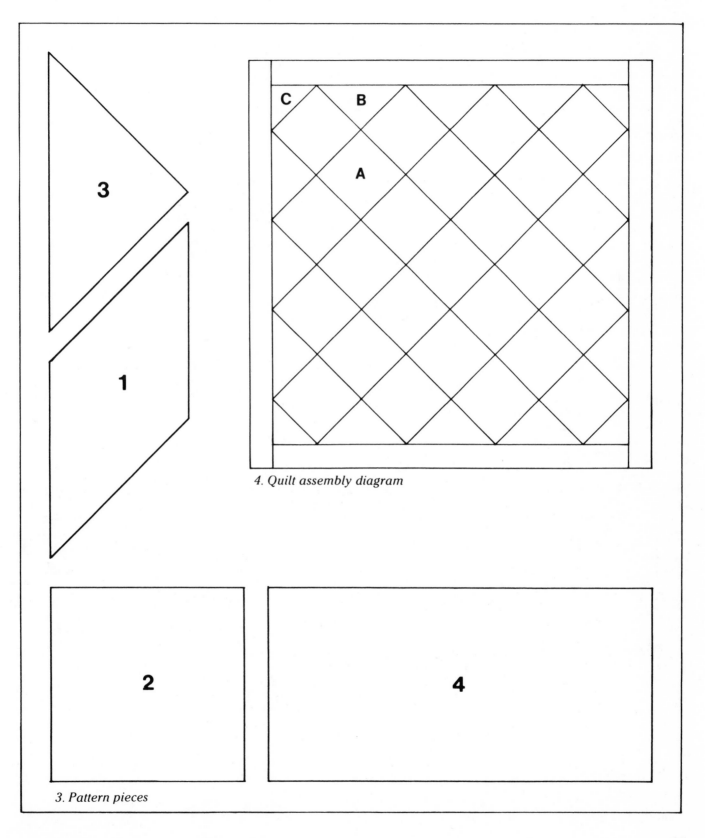

3

1

C B

A

2

4

4. Quilt assembly diagram

3. Pattern pieces

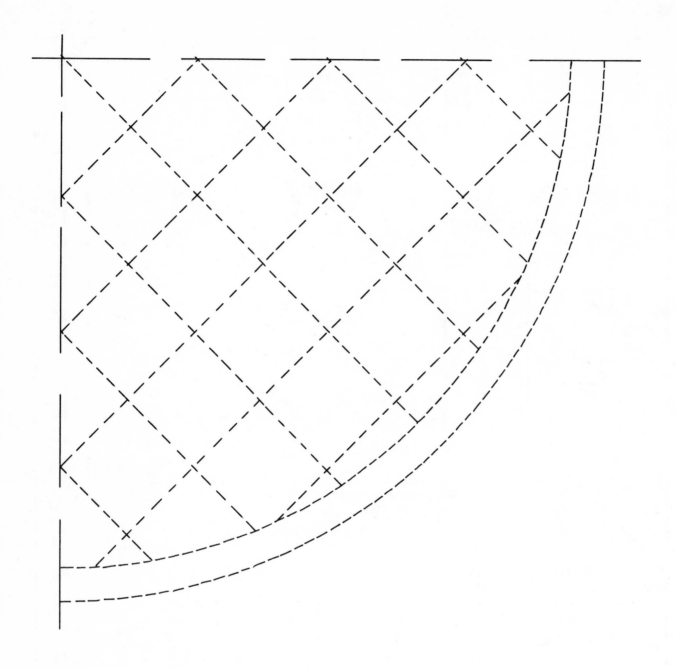

5. Quilting pattern

5. Quilting pattern

Baskets and Lattice Grid

This quilt is an example of the traditional basket design done in a 2-color scheme of red and white. You've probably seen this design done many different ways—with printed fabric or with two solid contrasting colors against a white background. If you look carefully, you may be able to see that some of the baskets have been signed with sayings and names. This often was a quiltmaker's whim.

The blocks can be made entirely by piecing, or you can combine piecing with appliqué, which is the way it is done here.

This finished quilt is 88 x 96 inches, which is a good size for a queen-size or double bed. The lattice strips are 1½ inches wide.

Materials
7⅔ yards red fabric
7⅔ yards white fabric
batting and backing material

Directions
___

The quilt is made up of 66 blocks and 25 partial blocks around the border. Note that the partial blocks are not all identical, so refer to the photograph when piecing.

Begin by tracing the pattern pieces and transferring them to heavy paper in order to cut templates (see page 17). When cutting fabric, add ¼-inch seam allowance.

To make one block

Each finished block is 9 x 9 inches. Cut 78 white fabric squares 9½ x 9½ inches. To make one block, fold fabric in half diagonally and make a crease. This will enable you to find the center of the fabric.
1. The basket is made up of rows of pieced triangles. With right sides together and edges aligned, join #1 and #2 pieces. Alternating red and white, make a row of 7 pieces.
2. Beginning again with a red #1 triangle, join 5 pieces. The next row is made up of a red, white, and red triangle.
3. Join a #3 piece as indicated on #1 block diagram.

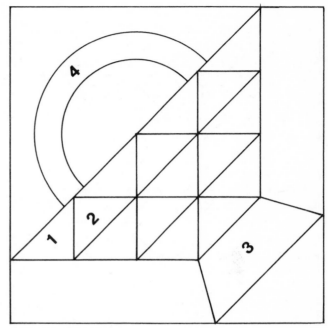

1. Block diagram

piece no.	in each block	in quilt*
1	9	708
2	6	502
3	1	84
4	1	86

*Total includes pieces in partial edge blocks

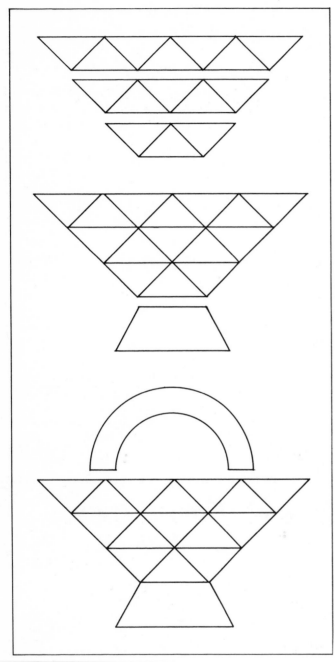

2. Block assembly diagram

Preparing the appliqué

It is difficult to make a curved shape lie flat on the fabric, but this is the goal in appliqué (piece #4). It will help if you work in a hoop so that the fabric is taut. Cotton will hold the turned edges better than a blend.

1. Stay-stitch ¼ inch from each curved edge of handle.
2. Clip the curves, turn on stitching line, and press.
3. Join handle to pieced basket in the following way: Find center of top edge of basket. With right sides together, pin each handle edge to basket and stitch across at these points.
4. Press all seams toward center of the basket.
5. Press seam-allowance edges of basket toward center.

Joining basket to block

1. Place the pieced basket on the center of the block and pin in position.
2. Using red thread and a #8 Sharp needle, appliqué the basket to the background with a blind, overcast, or running stitch. For the quilt shown here, a blind stitch was used.

Making border blocks

Cut 11 white fabric squares in half on the diagonal. Cut the remaining square in half and in half again to create the bottom corners.

Refer to diagram for piecing half-basket blocks and top and bottom partial blocks.

Joining blocks

Begin by cutting the sashes from the red fabric. All sashes are 2½ inches wide (including seam allowance). Cut 79 strips 9½ inches long. Cut one each in the following lengths:

132 inches
121 inches
97 inches
75 inches
53 inches
31 inches
108 inches
86 inches

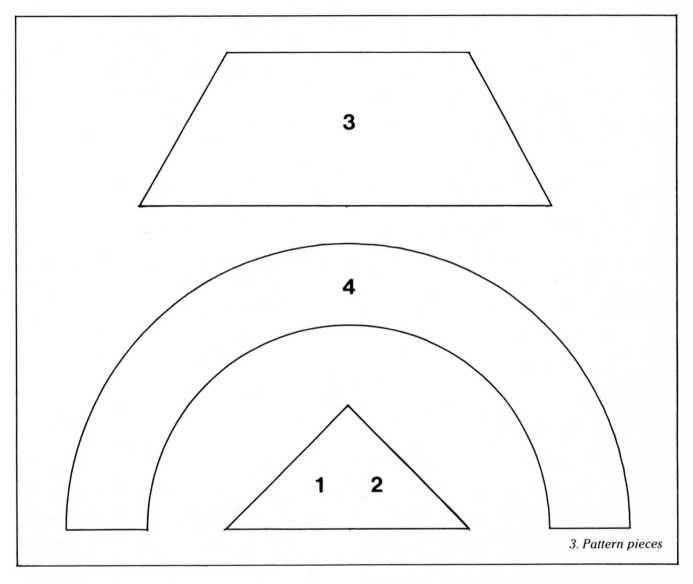

3. Pattern pieces

64 inches
42 inches
20 inches
12 inches

Refer to #4 quilt assembly diagram for joining blocks to make separate rows. The long sashes are used to join all rows.

Quilting

Baste the backing, batting, and top together before quilting. Take small running stitches on either side of all seams. Do the same along the lattice seams. You can use red thread on the sashes and white on the background, or use white everywhere. It is often preferable to see the stitches, but this is a matter of choice.

If you want to do more quilting, you can create a 1-inch-square grid pattern on the background of each block (see page 23).

When all quilting is complete, cut away the basting stitches and finish the edges.

To finish

There is a 1-inch red border around the edge of the quilt. This is created from the backing material, which is folded over and brought forward, then stitched to the top (see page 20).

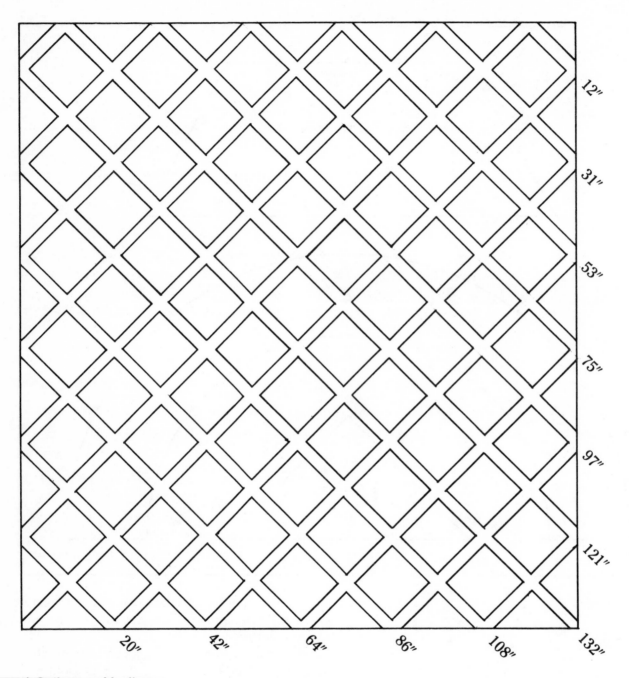

12"

31"

53"

75"

97"

121"

132"

20" 42" 64" 86" 108"

4. Quilt assembly diagram

This quilt is also known as the Virginia Lily and the Double Tulip. The design is composed of diamonds and triangles and combines piecing and appliqué. Notice in the color plate that, the way the red and green calico prints are placed, every row reverses.

Each set of flowers completely fills a block, which is 11 x 11 inches. There are 32 blocks. The finished quilt is 85 x 101 inches, which will fit a ·double or a queen-size bed.

Materials

2⅔ yards red printed fabric, such as calico
2⅔ yards green printed or solid fabric
7 yards white fabric
batting and backing material

Directions

Trace and transfer each pattern piece to heavy paper to cut templates (see pages 17, 18–19). Remember that the stems, #8 and #9, and the leaves, #10, are appliqués, while the other pattern pieces are pieced. When cutting the fabric, leave a ¼-inch seam allowance.

Prepare the appliqué pieces (see page 20). Turn all edges under and press. (See page 19 for curved appliqué pieces.) You can use bias tape for thè stems if desired, or you might find that stay-stitching along seam lines makes turning the edges easier. Use the templates to turn and press down edges as well.

To make one block

Refer to #1 block diagram when piecing sections. There are 12 A blocks and 20 B blocks.
1. To make the flower, piece four #1 sections together, as shown.
2. Join piece #2 to the base of the flower section.
3. Piece two #4 triangles between #1 points as indicated on diagram.
4. Piece a #3 square between center points to complete flower square. This is Unit X.
5. Repeat steps one and two. Refer to Unit Y and piece #3 square in position. Next, add #4 triangles between remaining points #1. This completes Unit Y.

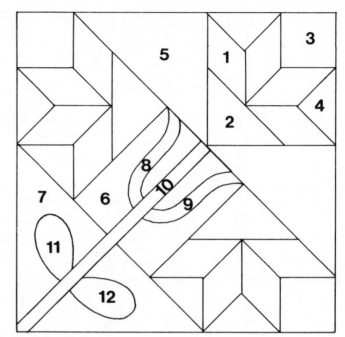

1. Block diagram

12 A blocks: red stems, green leaves
20 B blocks: green stems, red leaves
(32 pieced blocks total)

piece no.	in each block	in quilt
1R	12	144
1G	12	240
2R	3	36
2G	3	60
3	3	96
4	6	192
5	2	64
6	1	32
7	1	32
8R	2	24
8G	2	40
9R	2	24
9G	2	40
10R	1	12
10G	1	20
11R	1	12
11G	1	20
12R	1	12
12G	1	20
13 white triangle		148
14 green triangle		74
15 red triangle		74
White half squares		14
White quarter squares		4

6. Repeat steps one and two. Refer to Unit Z and join triangles #4 and square #3 in position as shown. This completes Unit Z. It is important that the piecing sequence be correct.

7. With right sides together and edges aligned, join piece #5 to Unit X. Join another piece #5 to the opposite side to make a piece in the shape of a triangle.

8. Join Unit Z and Unit Y to either side of piece #6.

9. With right sides together and edges aligned, join piece #7 to one long edge of pieced section Z-6-Y as shown.

10. Join remaining section to top edge of the piece.

11. Pin #10 stem in position on background. Pin #8 and #9 stems where indicated with edges tucked under #10 stem.

12. Position and pin each #11 and #12 leaf on either side of stem #10 as shown. Blindstitch all appliqué edges.

Joining blocks

There is a row of plain half blocks around the inside border with a quarter block in each corner. To make these triangle shapes, with an accurate measure draw an 11- x 11-inch square on a piece of plain paper. Fold in half on the diagonal and cut on the crease.

Use the paper pattern as your template to cut 14 plain white fabric squares, adding a ¼-inch seam allowance all around.

Fold the paper pattern in half again on the diagonal. Cut along the crease. Use this pattern to cut 4 white fabric triangles with an added ¼-inch seam allowance. These are your corner pieces.

1. Follow the quilt layout and join a corner triangle to the edge of one block. Open seams and press.

2. Join a border triangle to either side of the pieced block as shown. It's important to refer to the layout to see the position of each pieced block.

3. The next row will have a border triangle, then 3 pieced blocks, followed by a border triangle.

4. Continue to join blocks to make rows of blocks. Each pieced block is a reverse of the one next to it. In other words; you will begin each row with an A block, followed by a B block, etc.

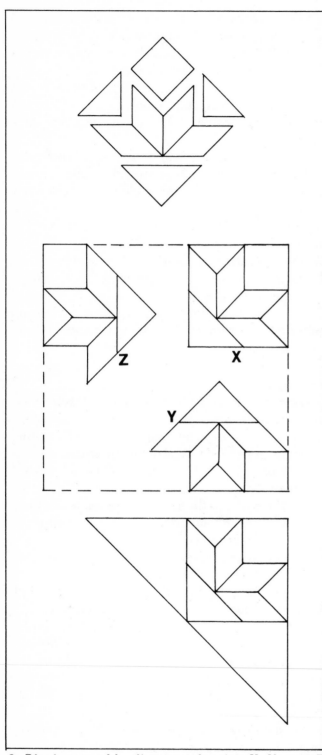

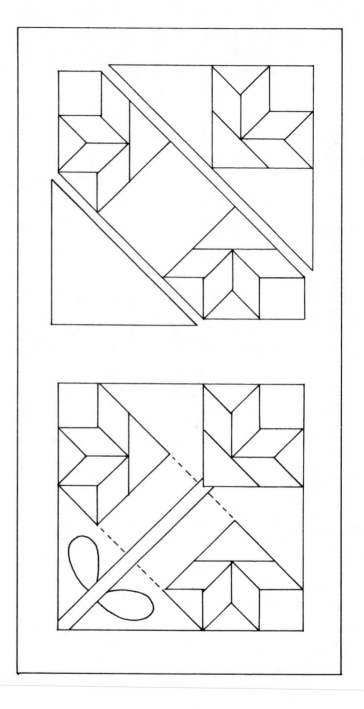

2. Block assembly diagram showing X, Y, and Z units

5. Join all rows according to the layout. Open seams and press.

Making borders

The inside border is made up of a #14 green or a #15 red triangle pieced to a #13 white triangle to form little boxes that are then pieced together. Refer to color plate.

1. When you have created two strips of pieced boxes measuring 62 inches long and 2 strips 83 inches long, join with quilt top for inside border.
2. Cut 2 strips of white fabric 9½ x 64 inches and 2 strips 9½ x 85 inches for the outside border.
3. With right sides together, align top border piece with top of quilt and stitch along edge. Repeat on the bottom.
4. Join long strips to each side of quilt in the same way. There will be extra fabric to trim when overlapping corners (see page 20).

Quilting

There are several ways to quilt the blocks and borders. You can outline each pieced patch and appliqué pieces with running stitches, or mark diagonal lines across the entire quilt inside the borders as shown here.

1. Trace and transfer the quilting pattern for each plain triangle.
2. The feathered pattern (see pages 90–91) is used on the wide outside border. Transfer it to the border so that it forms a continuous pattern that meets gracefully at each corner.
3. Cut backing and batting same size as quilt top.
4. Baste all 3 layers together with batting between.
5. Quilt along premarked lines with small, closely spaced running stitches. Stitch along all inside border pieced seams. Do not quilt through outside-edge seam allowance.

To finish

Trim batting back and turn edges from backing material and top toward the inside. Slip-stitch the folds together.

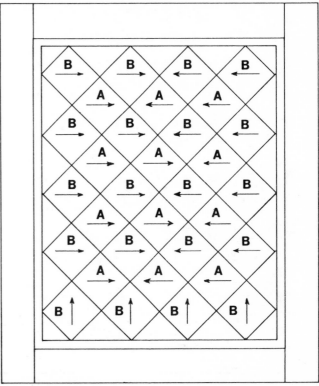

4. Quilt assembly diagram
Arrows indicate direction of design
"A" and "B" indicate color scheme of block

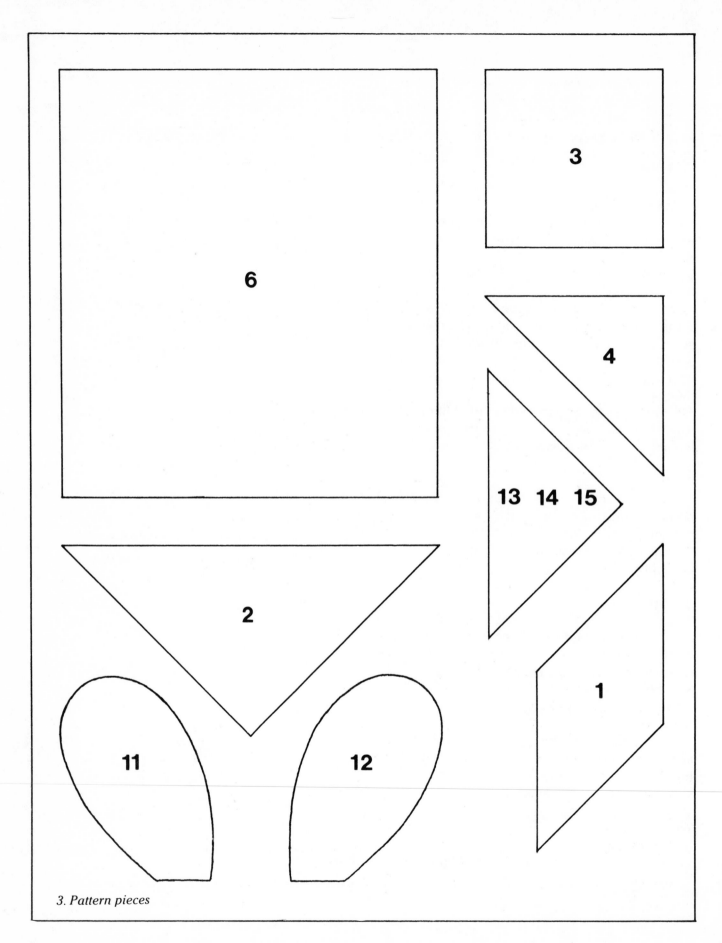

3. Pattern pieces

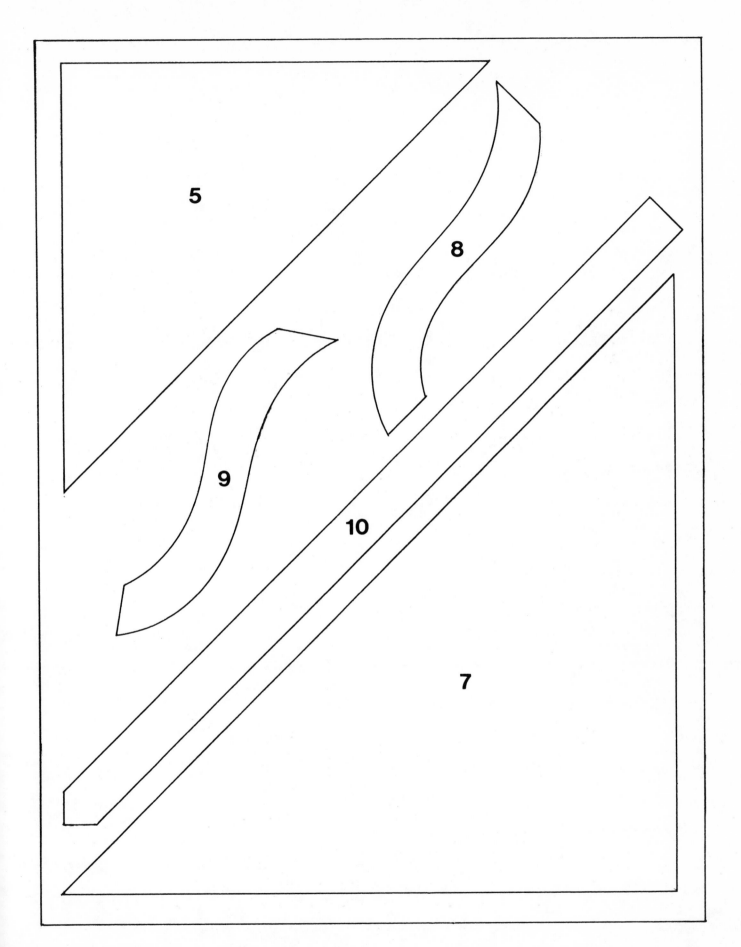

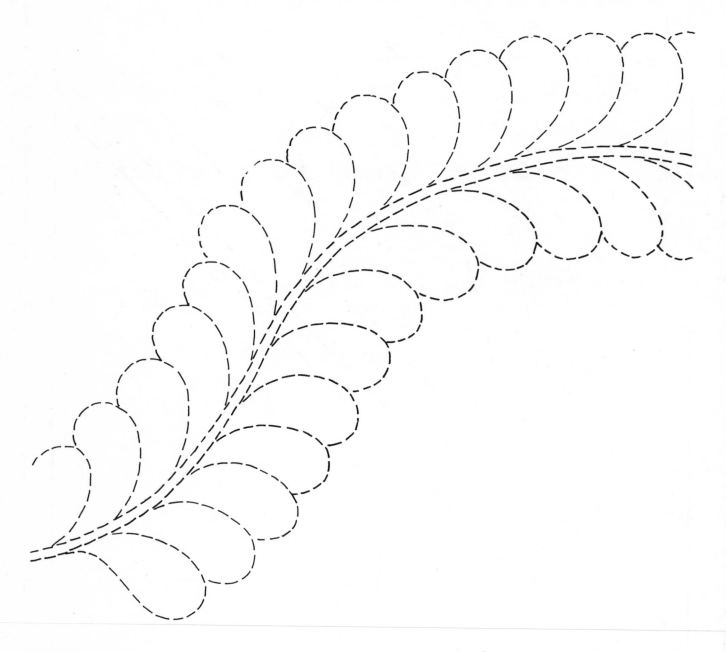

5. Quilting pattern

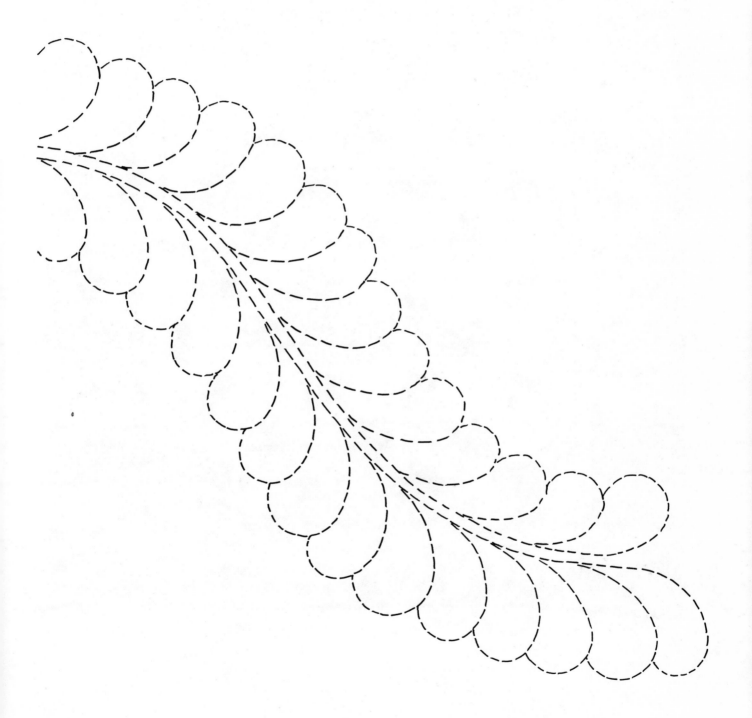

Checkered Stars

Made from red, black, and yellow calico, this checkerboard pattern is a popular version of the Le Moyne Star. The alternating white blocks are quilted in a pinwheel pattern, and the wide border is heavily quilted as well.

This quilt makes a very impressive wall hanging, as it measures 90 inches square. It will fit a queen-size bed. For twin size, make 6 blocks across, including the white blocks, and 9 blocks down as shown. The border is 11 inches wide. If you want to make this project for a king-size bed, add the necessary inches to the border.

Materials
1 yard black printed fabric
2 yards red printed fabric
5⅔ yards yellow printed fabric
2⅔ yards white fabric
batting and backing material

Directions

There are 40 pattern blocks and 41 white blocks. Each block is 7 x 7 inches. Begin by tracing and transferring the pattern pieces to heavy cardboard to make a template for each (see pages 18–19). When cutting out pieces, refer to chart for the number of pieces in each color. Add ¼-inch seam allowance when cutting. The patterns are given for the sewing lines, not cutting lines.

To make one block
1. Refer to #1 block assembly diagram for sequence of joining pieces. With right sides together and seams aligned, piece contrasting diamonds #1 and #2 to make up the star.
2. Join triangle pieces #3 between center points of star.
3. Piece squares #4 in each corner between points to complete the block. Open seams and press. Make 40.

Joining blocks
1. Cut out 41 squares of white fabric 7½ x 7½ inches.

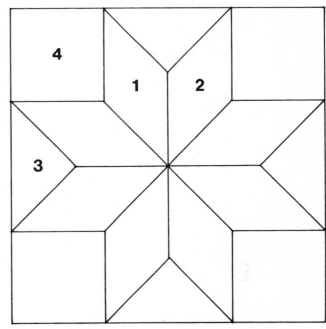

1. Block diagram

piece no.	in each block	in quilt
1	4	160
2	4	160
3	4	160
4	4	160
border		
5		120
6		120

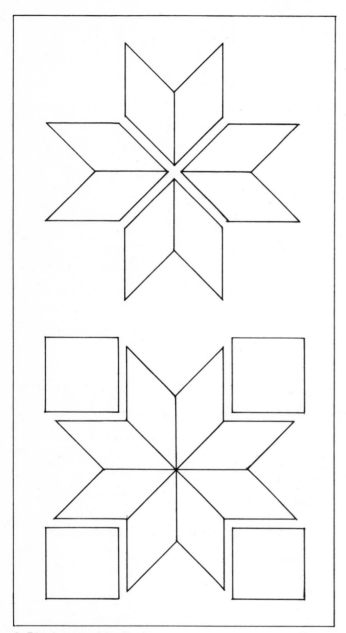

2. Block assembly diagram

2. Beginning with a white square, join with a pattern block. Continue to do this, alternating blocks until you have a row of 9 blocks.

3. Begin the next row with a pattern block and make the next alternating row. Piece together 9 separate rows of blocks in this way.

4. With right sides together and seams aligned, join rows. Open seams and press.

Making narrow border

1. The narrow borders are 2 inches wide. Piece together the number of triangles, alternating #5 red and #6 yellow fabric according to diagram #4 quilt assembly.
2. Make 4 separate strips and join top and bottom pieces, then side strips.

Making wide border

Cut 2 strips of yellow fabric 11½ x 92 inches and 2 strips 11½ x 69 inches. I've added 2 inches to the length of each strip. This can be cut to fit after the borders are joined. If there is any shrinkage or shifting of size, it's always better to have a couple of inches to work with.

This border has overlapping corners (see page 20).

Quilting

1. Trace and transfer the quilting pattern onto each white block as indicated. Do the same for the wide border design.
2. Baste the 3 layers of material together with the batting between. Take small running stitches on either side of each seam on the pieced blocks. Do this along the premarked quilting pattern in each white block and around the border.

To finish

The 1-inch-wide edging is made from the contrasting red fabric, which is also used for the backing. You can do one of two things. Either cut the backing material 2 inches larger than the front in order to bring it forward as a finish (see page 21), or you can make a bias strip that is a separate piece to be applied after the quilt is finished (see pages 21–22).

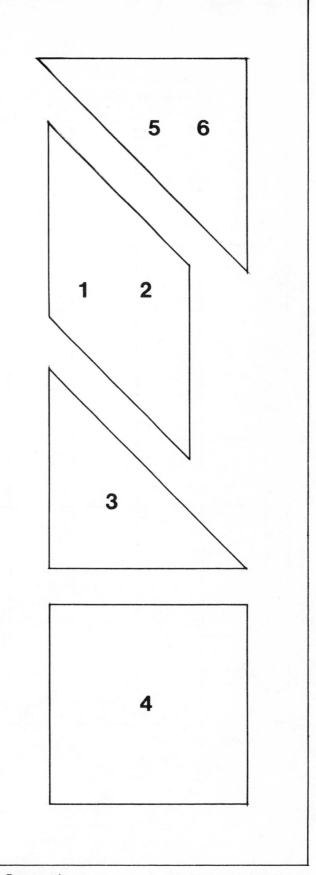

3. Pattern pieces

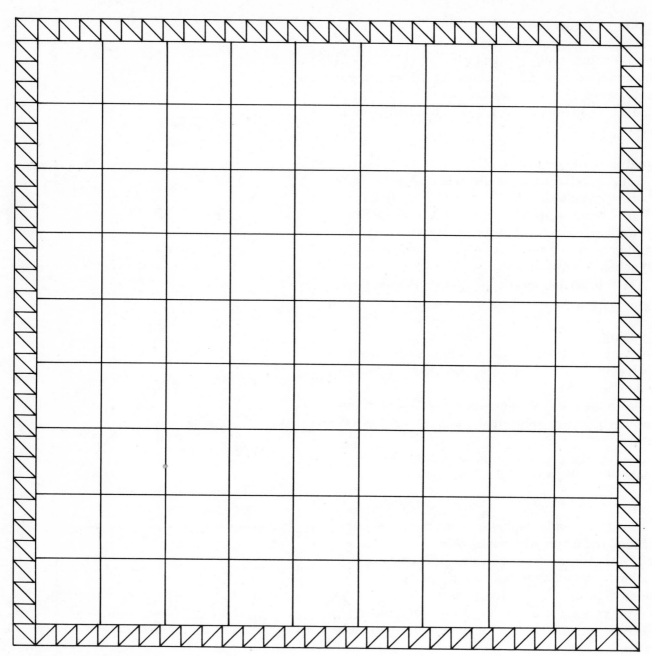

4. Quilt assembly diagram

Carolina Lily

Maple Star

Rose and Bud

Teacup

Rolling Stone

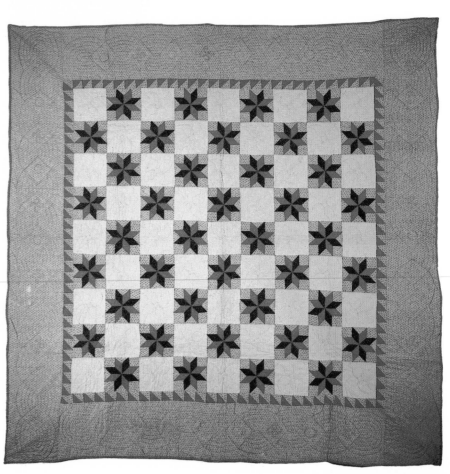

Checkered Stars

Broken Star

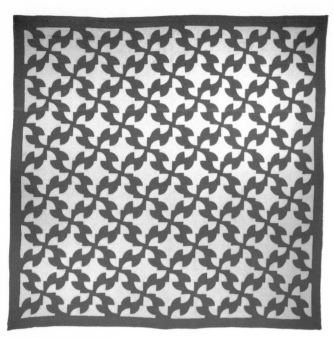

Drunkard's Path

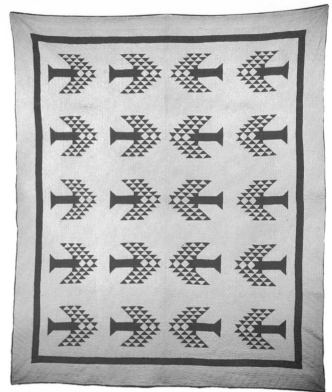

Tree of Life

Alphabet Quilt

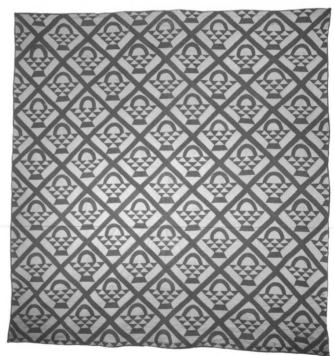

Baskets and Lattice

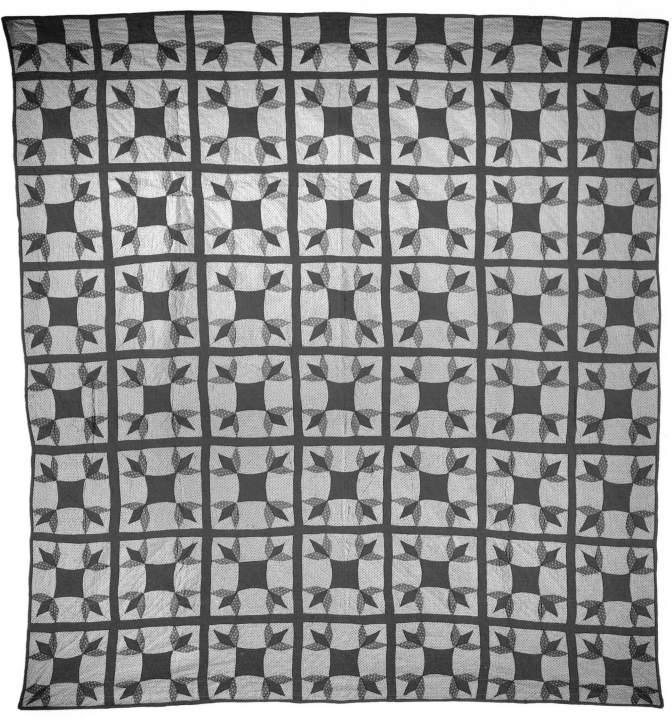

Turkey Tracks

Log Cabin (Pineapple)

Log Cabin (Barn Raising)

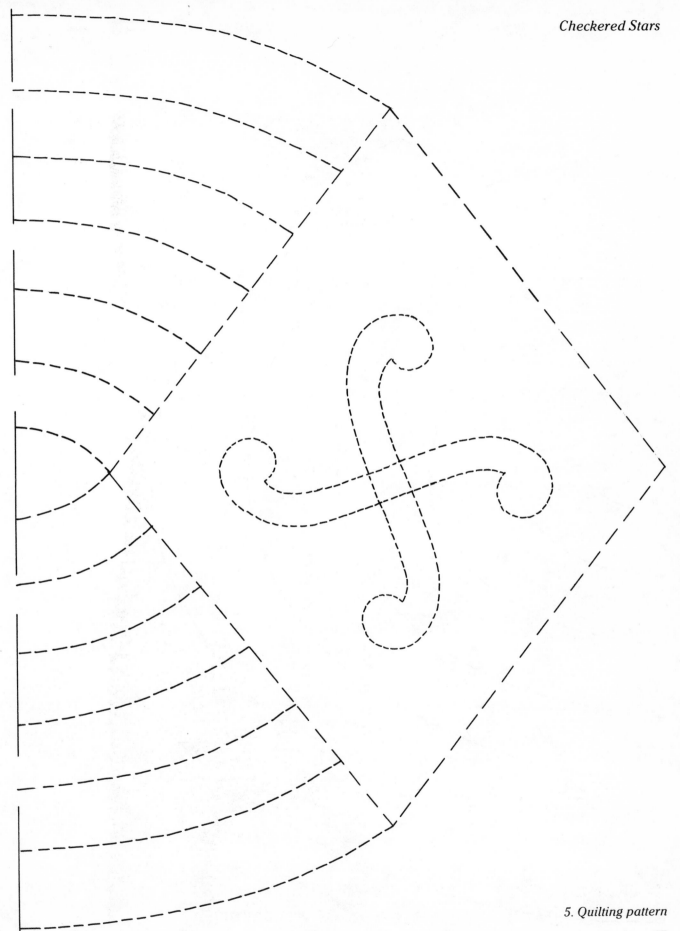

5. Quilting pattern

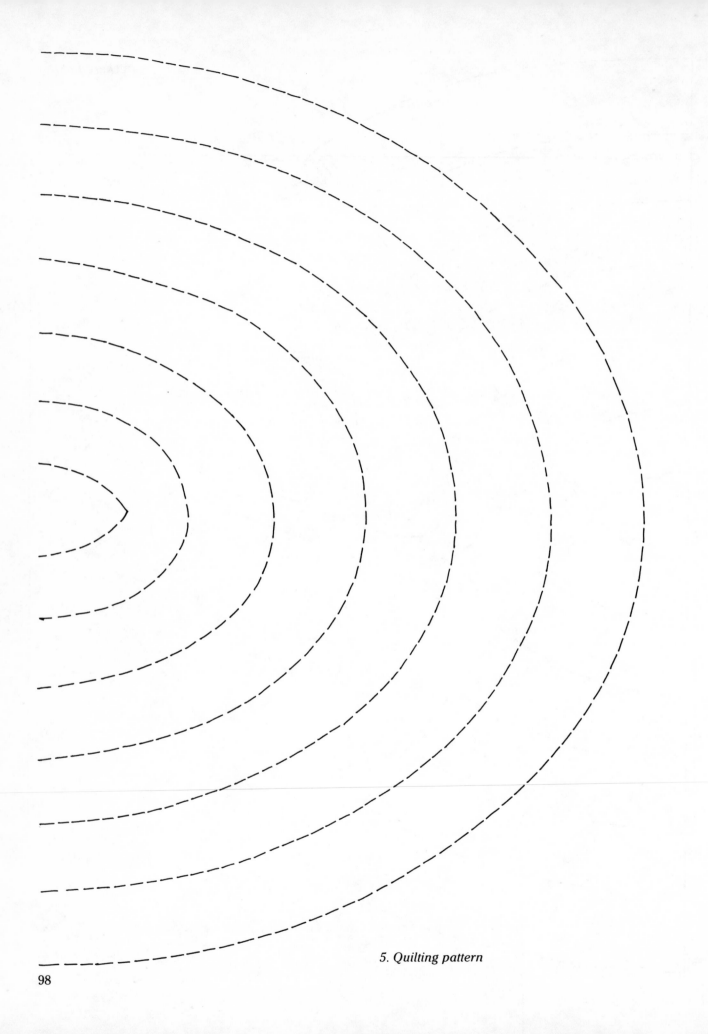

5. Quilting pattern

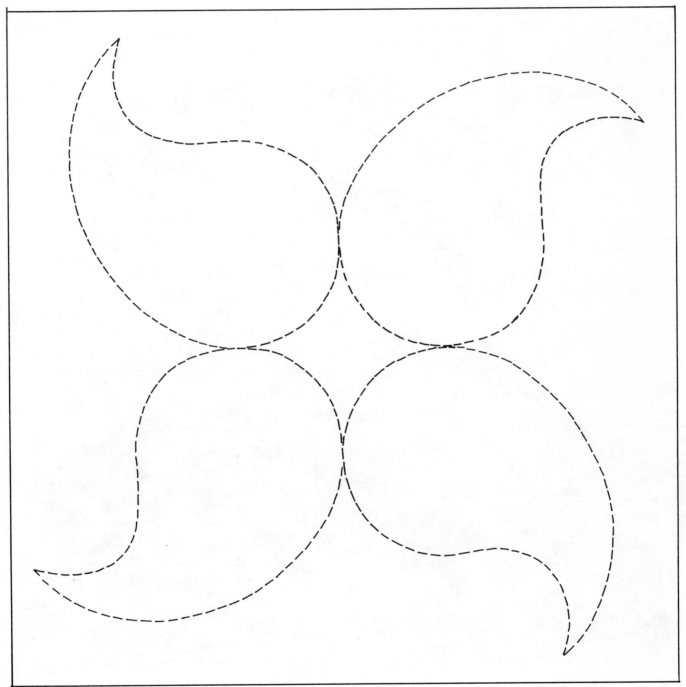

5. Quilting pattern

Star of Bethlehem

This pattern is one of the most popular one-patch designs used in quiltmaking. This means that the same shape is repeated to make the overall design and is seen in many variations of color combinations. It is often called by different names, among them Sunburst and Lone Star.

Made entirely of diamond shapes, the star is often used as a repeated design or as one large design for a dramatic effect. It is important to take special care when choosing and placing the colors. This finished quilt is 84 x 84 inches, which will fit a double or queen-size bed. For better coverage on the length, add 6 inches to top and bottom border.

Materials
1 yard rose fabric
1⅓ yards gold fabric
1 yard yellow fabric
1⅓ yards red fabric
1 yard light blue fabric
1⅓ yards dark blue fabric
1⅔ yards pink fabric
2⅔ yards light print for background and borders
batting and backing material

Directions

Making the Star
When piecing this quilt, you will notice that the large star in the center and each corner star are made up of 8 diamond-shaped sections. These sections are pieced together to form the star.
1. Trace and transfer the diamond shape to template material. You will need 1,232 pieces.
2. Refer to the chart and cut the number of diamonds from each fabric color. Remember to leave a ¼-inch seam allowance when cutting each piece.
3. *Note:* The pieces are long diamonds that require accurate cutting and piecing. Machine sewing is the easiest method for piecing this quilt. When sewed together, the 8 points of each segment must meet so that the quilt will lie flat.

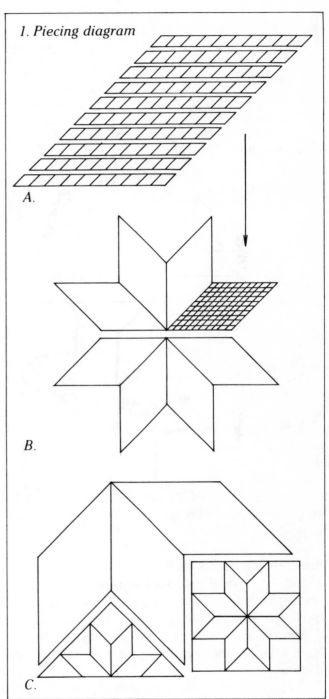

1. Piecing diagram

A. 10 rows of 10 patches make 1 large diamond section
B. Join halves of large star
C. Piece #8 and #9 patches around small stars, then join to large star

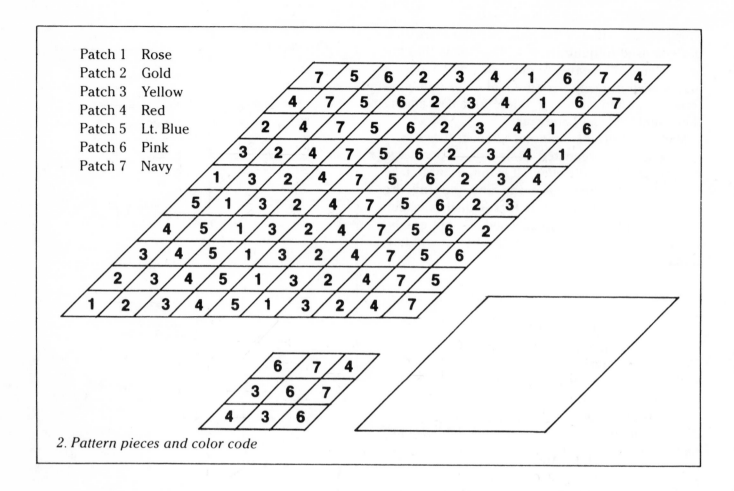

Patch 1   Rose
Patch 2   Gold
Patch 3   Yellow
Patch 4   Red
Patch 5   Lt. Blue
Patch 6   Pink
Patch 7   Navy

2. Pattern pieces and color code

4. Refer to diagrams #1 and #2 and make up 10 rows of 10 diamond patches in the color sequence indicated.

Assembling patchwork

1. Join 10 rows of patches and repeat for each of the separate 8 diamond shapes that will make up the larger star. Follow color key for sequence.

2. Join the star together in separate halves so you have 2 large pieces made up of 4 segments (see diagram #1).

3. With right sides together, join top and bottom halves of the star.

4. Following the color key for sequence, make the 4 small corner stars by piecing 3 rows of 3 diamond shapes 8 times. Join as with large center star.

5. Make up 4 half stars with 4 points consisting of 9 diamonds in each.

piece no.	in quilt
1	88
2	136
3	224
4	248
5	112
6	232
7	192
8 square	20
9 triangle	32

102

4. Quilt assembly diagram

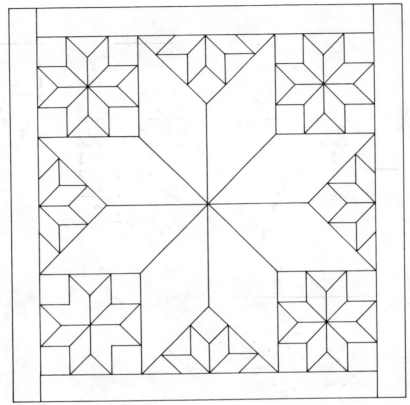

Joining with background

To join all stars, you can either continue to piece each element or appliqué each completed section to the background fabric. This quilt was pieced, and the following directions are for this method. (For appliqué, see page 20.)

1. The small stars are joined at each corner with a #8 background square 6 x 6 inches and between each of the 4 remaining points with a #9 triangle (2 sides, 6 inches each). You will now have 4 blocks with a small star in the center.

2. To make the half blocks, piece a #8 square of background fabric to one side of a point, then fold the half star in half with right sides together and join the next sides. Repeat with the 4 triangles that go between the remaining points.

3. Join blocks to the larger star.

To finish

The border of this quilt is made from the fabric used as the background for the stars. However, you might like to use a color from the star, such as the dark blue, for the border.

1. Attach border pieces and finish corners by overlapping (see page 20).

2. Cut batting to fit quilt top.

3. Cut backing material and seam together (see page 18). The binding around the quilt edges can be made from the backing or can be a matching binding tape purchased where notions are sold. If you use the backing material, be sure to leave an extra 2 inches of fabric all around when cutting.

4. Baste the quilt top, batting, and backing together.

Quilting

The quilting here was done by hand. Take small running stitches along either side of each seam where the diamond pieces are patched together.

The border is not quilted. However, if you want quilting around this area, draw a grid or a pattern to be quilted (see page 23). Choose one of the border patterns from another quilt.

Peony Quilt

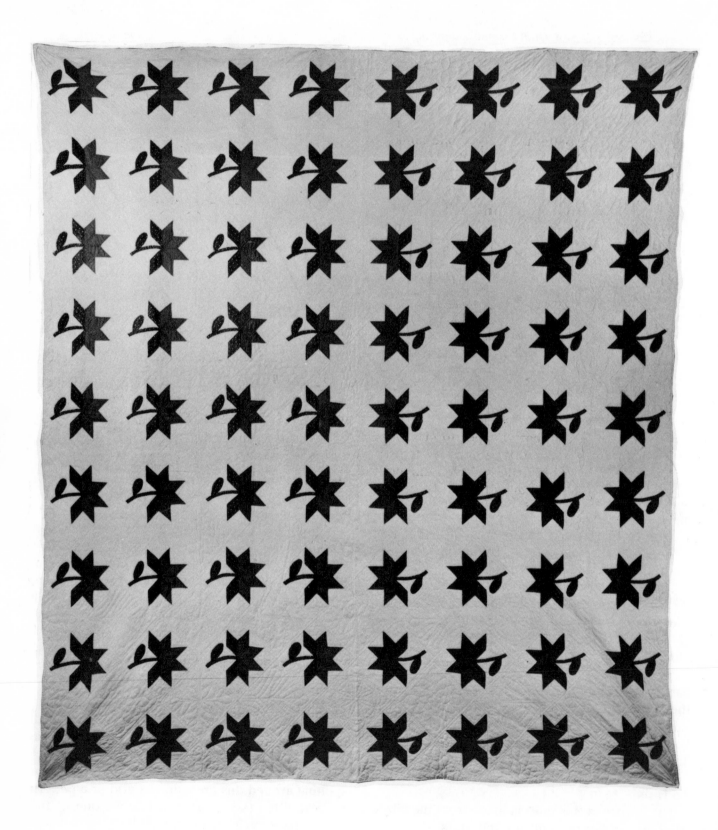

This is an excellent project for a beginner. The design is simple but appealing, and you can make any color combination to match your room and be sure that the finished project will look good. The technique is appliqué and piecing, and there are 4 different quilting patterns in the white squares. This makes a simple pattern quite elegant.

The finished quilt is 90 x 101 inches, which will fit a queen- or king-size bed. It is made of 72 pieced blocks with 8 across and 9 down. To make it fit a twin bed, make 6 blocks across and 9 down.

Materials
2 yards red calico fabric
2 yards green calico fabric
9 yards white fabric
batting and backing material

Directions

Each block is 8 x 8 inches. Trace and transfer each pattern piece to heavy paper to cut a template (see pages 18–19). When cutting the diamond pieces #1 and #2, add ¼-inch seam allowance. When cutting the stem #7 and leaf #6, you might want to add a ⅜-inch seam allowance for ease in turning edges.

To make one block
Refer to #1 block diagram when piecing the block.
1. With right sides together and edges aligned, join a #1 piece to another #1 piece. Add a #1 piece to either side of this pieced section to create the flower.
2. With right sides together, join a #2 piece to a #1 and another #2 piece to the other #1 (as per diagram) to add leaves.
3. Join a #3 piece as shown. In this step you are turning a corner, which can be done as follows: Machine stitch down one edge to corner. With the needle still in the fabric, lift presser foot and clip in seam allowance to needle. Lift needle and remove fabric.

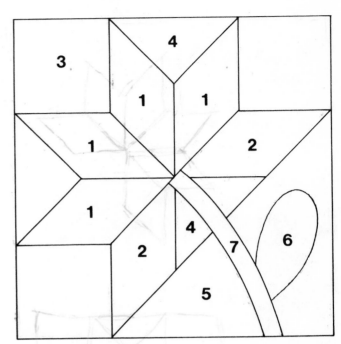

1. Block diagram

piece no.	in each block	in quilt
1	4	288
2	2	144
3	3	216
4	3	216
5	1	72
6	1	72
7	1	72
8 plain blocks		56
9 plain border triangles		30
10 plain corners		4

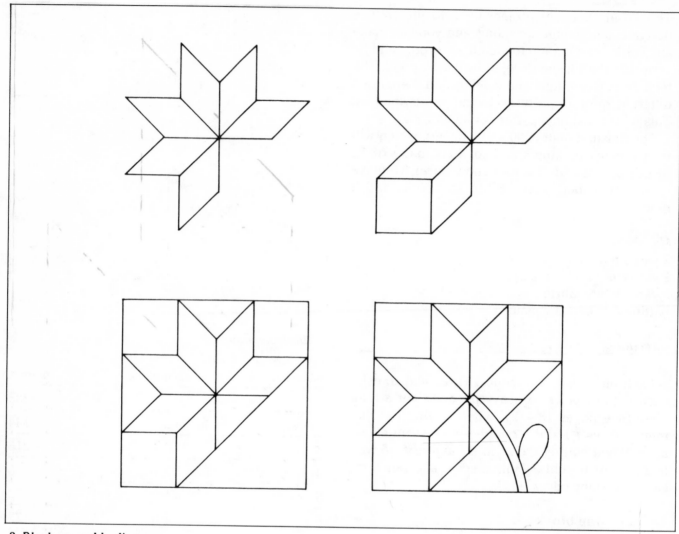

2. Block assembly diagram

Open piece so #3 is faceup. Fold down so #3 is facedown on #1 below it and raw edges are aligned. Stitch across to clipped corner. Press so fabric will lie flat. Repeat where #3 joins #1 and #2 points of flower.

4. Piece three #4 triangles in position.

5. Piece one #5 triangle to the bottom of the flower to complete the square.

6. Turn long edges of #7 under and press. Turn curved edge of #6 under and press (see page 19 for curved appliqué).

7. Turn the end of the stem piece #7 under where it will be attached to the flower, and press. Pin in place on the block.

8. Slip base of leaf #6 under stem, and pin to block.

9. Stitch appliqué pieces with a blind or a slip stitch.

The block is complete.

Making plain blocks

1. Cut 56 #8 squares of white fabric 8½ x 8½ inches.

2. Cut 15 of the blocks in half on the diagonal to make 30 #9 triangles to use around the border. There will be no seam allowance on the raw edges, which will be covered by the binding.

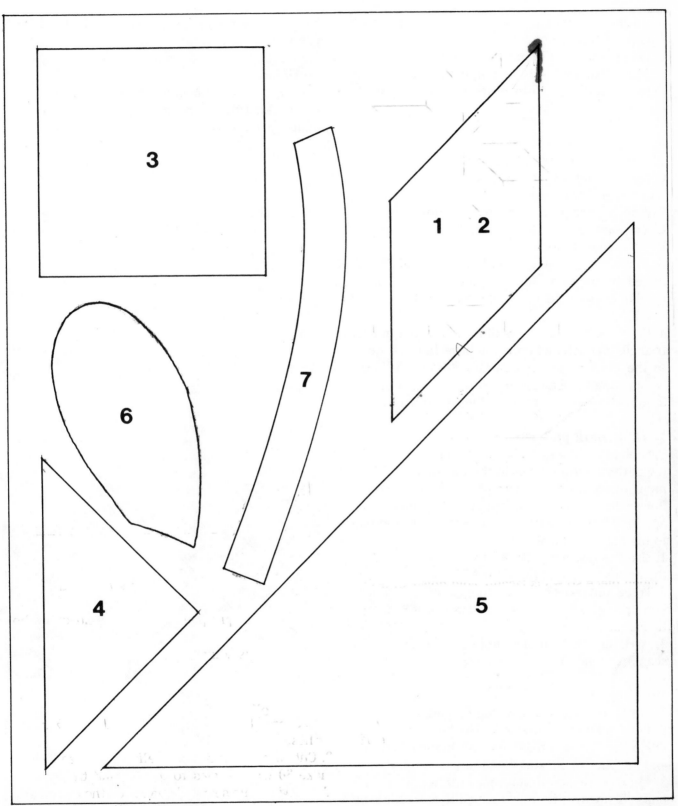

3. To make corner triangles, draw an 8- x 8-inch square on a piece of paper. Cut this in half on the diagonal and then in half again so you have 4 triangles. Use one #10 triangle to cut 4 fabric corners, adding a ¼-inch seam allowance when cutting.

Joining blocks

1. Refer to photograph for placement, and join one corner triangle to the top edge of one pieced block.
2. Join a border triangle to each opposite side. Open seams and press. You now have a corner and the first row of blocks.
3. Join a border triangle with a pieced block, followed by a plain block, a pieced block, and a border triangle to complete the second row of blocks.
4. Continue to make rows of blocks with a border triangle on each end until you have 16 rows. Refer to the quilt assembly diagram #4 so you know which rows have a corner triangle on one end.
5. Join all rows according to the layout diagram.

Marking quilt patterns

Each plain block and border triangle has a quilting pattern within. Refer to the diagram for placement of each design. The pieced blocks have a flower design in each square corner #3 piece. The appliquéd stem has a quilted leaf corresponding to the appliquéd leaf.

1. Use the leaf template #6 to outline the leaf on the opposite side of the stem #7.
2. Trace and transfer all quilting patterns to blocks and triangles. Repeat with patterns for pieced blocks.
3. Mark lines ½ inch on either side of each joining seam of each block.

Quilting

1. Cut batting same size as top of quilt.
2. Cut backing material 2 inches larger than top. Baste the 3 layers together with batting between and 2 inches of backing extending all around.
3. Quilt with small running stitches along all marked lines. Although this quilt was done by

hand, you can quilt each square on the machine if you want to save time.

To finish

Bring the extra backing material forward ¼ inch and press. Turn the remaining 1¼ inches over the quilt top and blindstitch to finish raw edges.

4. Quilt assembly diagram

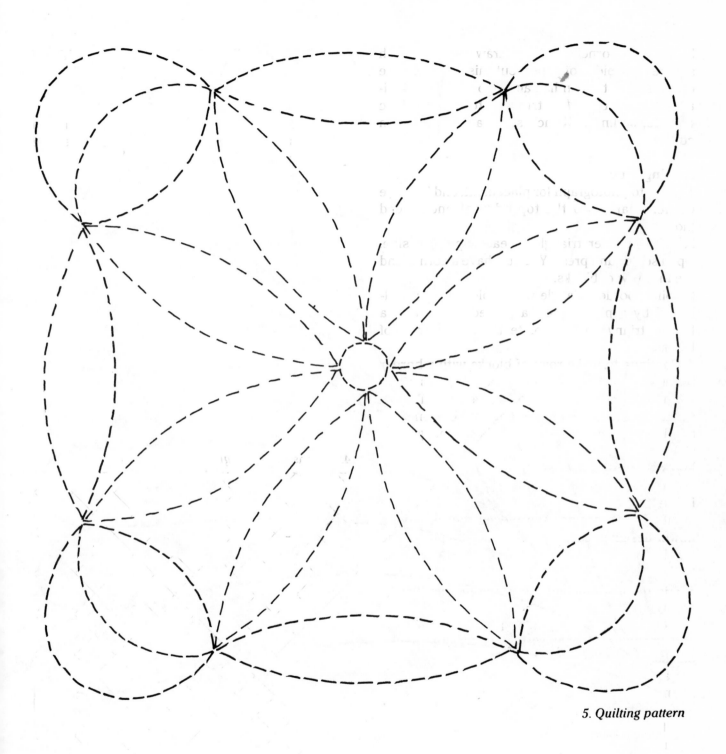

5. Quilting pattern

Peony Quilt

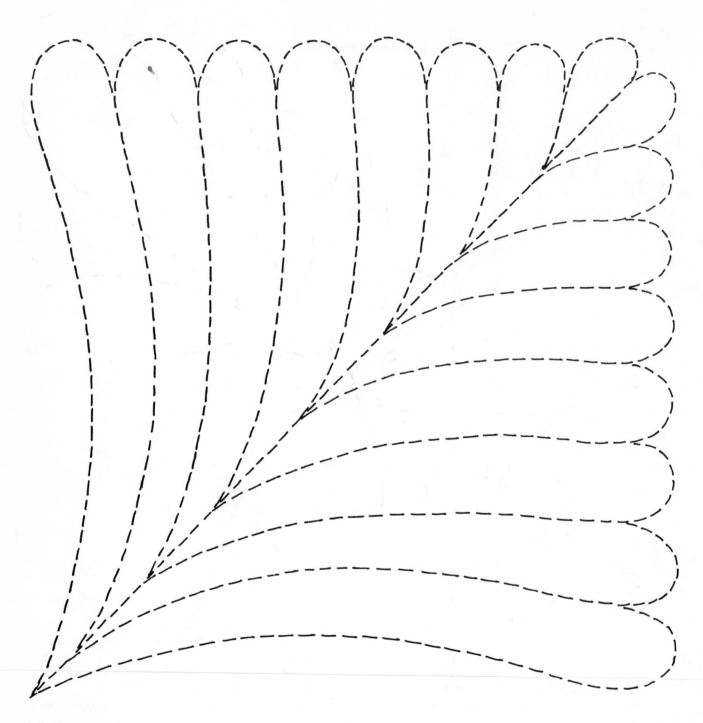

5. Quilting pattern

5. Quilting pattern

Mosaic Star

This quilt is made up of diamonds and hexagons. Some quiltmakers use the paper-pattern method for accuracy, but if you are careful, you can eliminate this procedure.

The colors used here are red, orange, and white. Choose the colors that best complement your room. The design will be just as effective if you use printed fabric.

The finished quilt is 88 x 108 inches and will fit a double or queen-size bed.

Materials

3 yards red fabric
3 yards orange fabric
8 yards white fabric
batting and backing material

Directions

Trace and transfer the pattern pieces to heavy paper to cut your templates (see pages 18–19). Refer to the chart when cutting the number of pieces from each color, and add ¼-inch seam allowance.

There is a lot of piecing to do, but since the quilt is all straight seams, there is nothing difficult about the pattern.

1. Refer to photograph for piecing sequence. Begin by piecing the individual stars. There are 68 complete stars and 4 half stars on top and bottom.
2. With right sides together and edges aligned, stitch 2 diamond pieces #1 together. If you are using 2 colors or prints for the stars, you will alternate each shape when piecing.
3. Piece all hexagons #2 together so you have 136 complete patches and 16 half patches.
4. Join pieces #3 between the points of each star.
5. The #4 pieces are used along the quilt edges. Although the shapes are irregular, you can still create rows, which are then joined to make up the quilt.

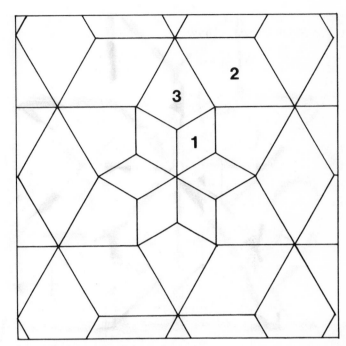

1. Block diagram

piece no.	in quilt
1	440
2	459
3	432
4	36

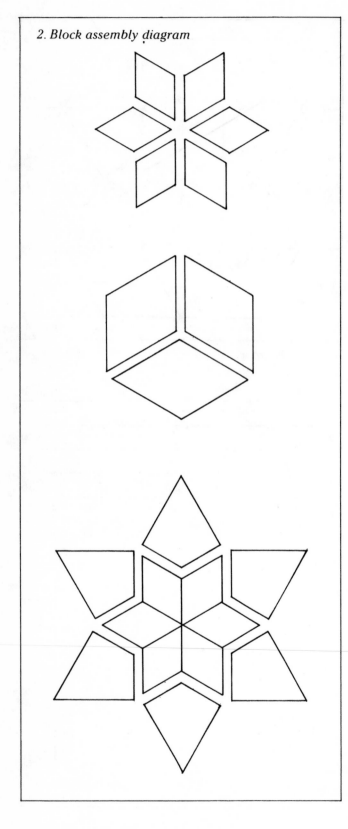

2. Block assembly diagram

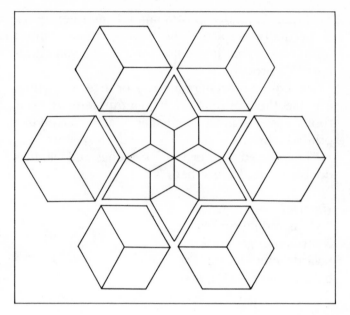

Quilting

1. Cut backing and batting same size as top if the edge is to have a bias trim (see page 65). However, if you want to have a narrow (1 inch) binding as shown here, cut the backing 2 inches larger than the quilt. After all quilting has been done, this extra piece is brought forward and stitched to the front edge of the quilt.

2. Baste the 3 layers together with the batting between. The quilting on the top follows the lines of the seams on all pieces. Take small running stitches.

3. Fold raw edge of backing forward ¼ inch and press all around. Fold again, over front edge of quilt, and stitch around to finish. Or, finish raw edges with bias tape.

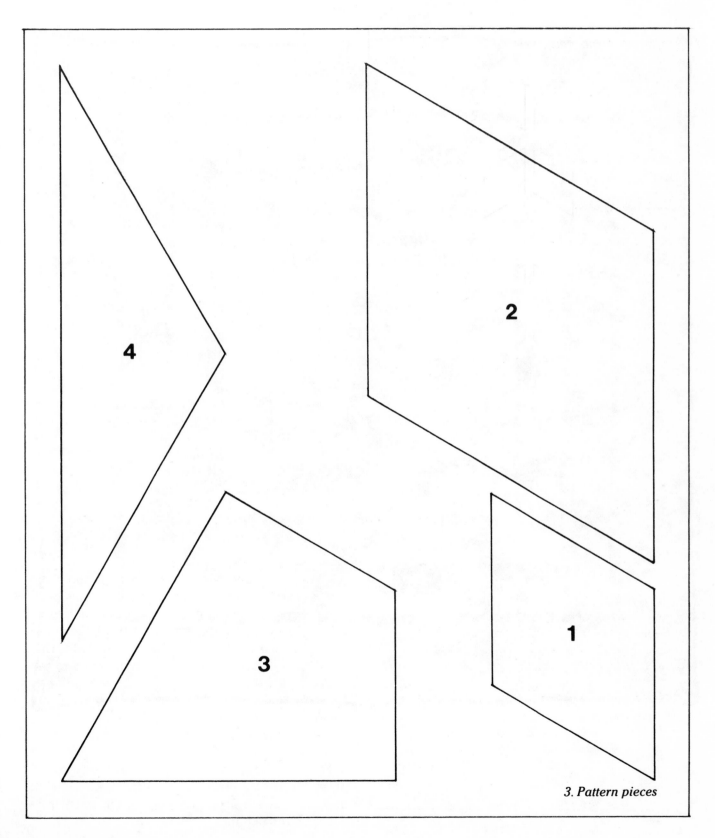

3. Pattern pieces

Delectable Mountains

This quilt pattern dates back to the eighteenth century. It has 4 rows of mountains encircling a star. The star is the familiar Le Moyne Star, of which you will find many examples throughout the book.

This is a nice example of a 2-color pattern with a heavily quilted wide border. It is entirely pieced. Shown here as a square wall hanging measuring 88 x 88 inches, it will fit a double or queen-size bed. You can add to the border if you need more length in order to bring it up and over the pillows.

Materials
2 yards navy blue dotted fabric (or print)
5⅔ yards white fabric
batting and backing material

Directions

The edge of this quilt is trimmed with bias binding made from the navy blue fabric (see pages 21–22). Plan to cut the strips for this first and then cut the pieces from what is left.

Trace and transfer each pattern piece to heavy paper to cut templates (see pages 18–19). Leave ¼-inch seam allowance when cutting fabric.

Piecing the sections
You will begin by piecing the center star and then piece each section around it. As you can see, this quilt is made up of identical pieces that form borders, each consisting of more mountains with triangles between. Refer to quilt assembly diagram #4.

1. To create the center star, make 3 pieced rows in the following way: With right sides together and edges aligned, join a #4 with a #2 piece. Next, join a #3 followed by #2 and #4 again.

2. Join a #2 with a #3 and a #2, as indicated on the diagram. Join this to one side of the center square piece #1. Repeat on the opposite side.

3. Make a row of #4 joined with #2 followed by #3, #2, and #4 again.

4. Piece all 3 rows together. The center block is complete. Open seams and press.

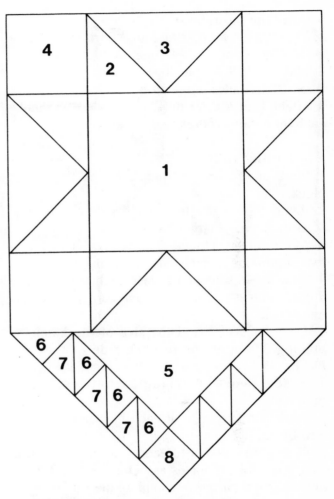

1. Center block and mountain unit

piece no.	in quilt
1	1
2	8
3	4
4	4
5	40
6	452
7	374
8	40
9	12
10	24

Making the mountains

1. Make Unit A by piecing four #6 triangles, three #7 triangles, and one #8 square into a strip.
2. Make Unit B by piecing four #6 triangles and three #7 triangles into a strip.
3. Attach Unit A and Unit B to triangle #5 to make each mountain. There are 40 mountains.

Assembling quilt

1. Piece one mountain to each side of the center block.
2. Piece a #9 triangle to each side' of the new square, making a larger block.
3. With right sides together and edges aligned, join two mountains to each side of the block.
4. Piece a #10 triangle between each mountain.
5. Piece four #9 triangles at each corner to make a new block.
6. Continue to expand the size of the block by piecing 3 mountains to each side of the new block.
7. Piece two #10 triangles between each mountain.
8. Piece a #9 triangle at each corner to make a new block.
9. Piece 4 mountains to each side of the square. Join three #10 triangles as before. Add a #9 triangle at each corner to complete the square.

Making inside borders

The narrow border that ties the block together in a frame is made up of 132 blue triangles pieced with 132 white triangles.

Refer to the photograph and piece, alternating triangles together to make the border strips. Join on each side with the quilt top.

Making outside borders

Cut 2 strips of white fabric 9½ x 90 inches and 2 strips 9½ x 72 inches. This measurement will give you an extra 2 inches in lengths, which you will trim after sewing.

Join top and bottom (short) strips first. Next, join side border strips and finish with overlapping corners (see page 20).

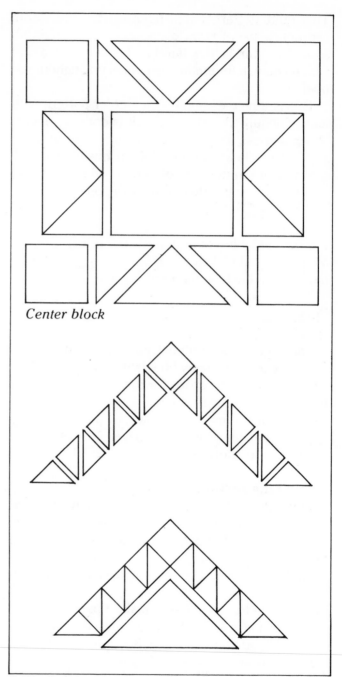

Center block

2. Block assembly diagram

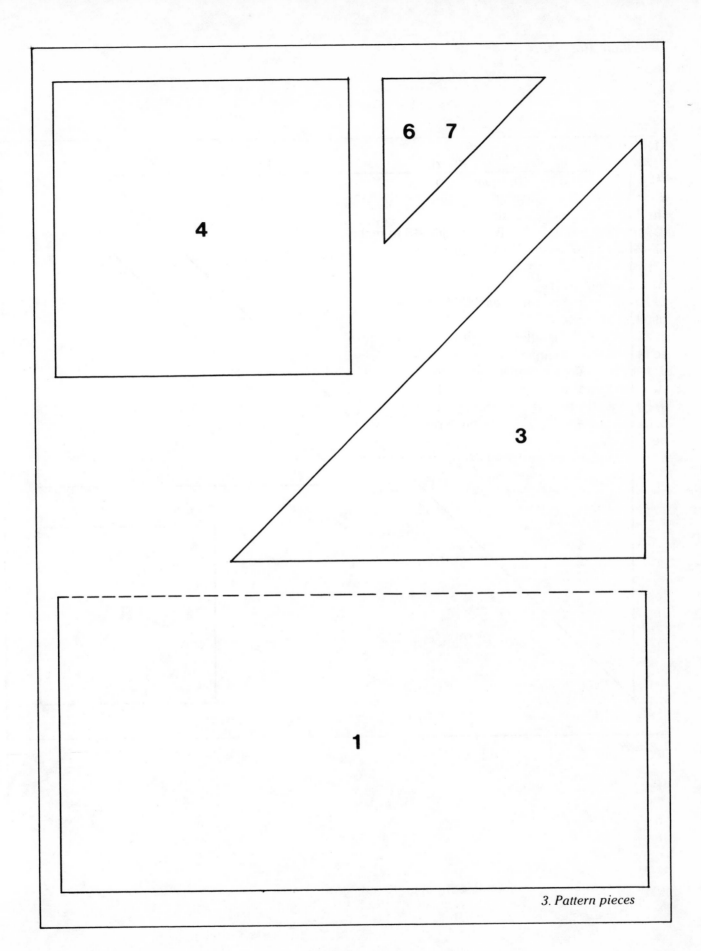

3. Pattern pieces

119

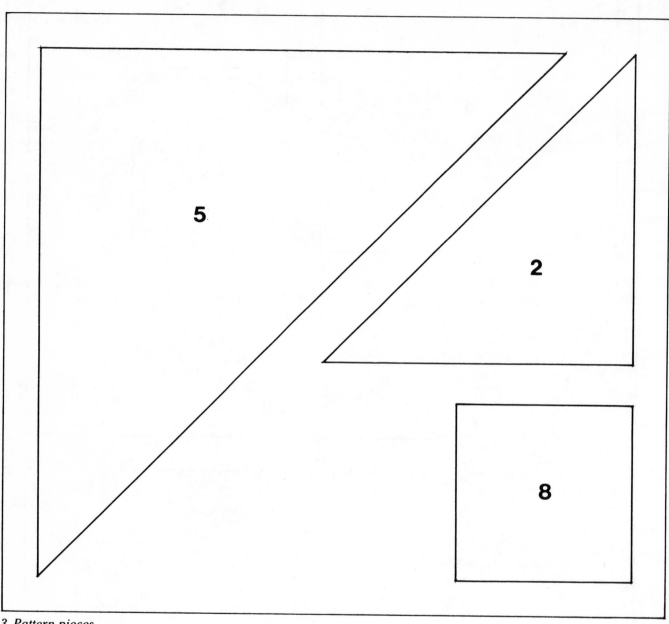

3. Pattern pieces

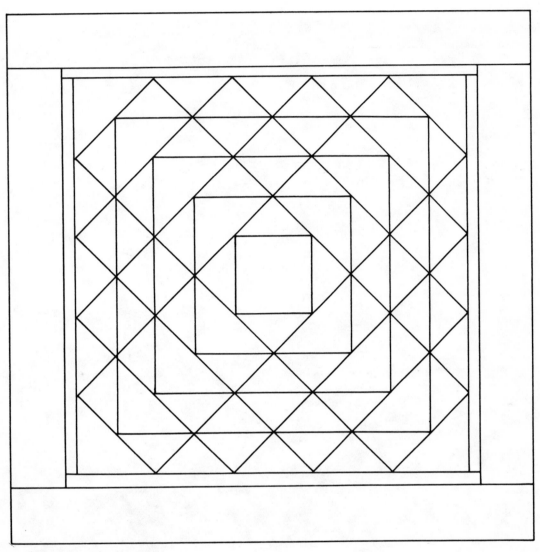

4. Quilt assembly diagram

Quilting

Mark entire quilt inside narrow border with a diamond grid. To do this, mark dividing lines from corner to corner. From these lines mark from center outward in evenly spaced lines.

Trace and transfer the feathered quilt design around the outside border. The design should be a continuous graceful curve all around.

Mark diagonal, evenly spaced lines across the border above and below the feathered pattern so that all white areas will be quilted.

Baste the 3 layers together (backing, batting, and top). Hand-stitch in small running stitches along all premarked quilting lines. Cut away basting stitches.

To finish

To finish the quilt with a bias binding, see pages 21−22 for directions. Whenever the binding goes around the corners, rather than squaring off, a bias strip is used. In this case the trim matches the pieced print, which gives the quilt a narrow band of navy blue that frames and defines the edge of the top.

Drunkard's Path

This basic design, a square with a curved shape in one corner, is often used as an example of what kind of variations are possible with a modular unit. The patterns we've provided show different ways you might rearrange the pieces.

Before beginning, refer to page 19 for basic directions that will help you when cutting curved pieces.

The finished quilt is 90 x 90 inches and is made up of 6 rows of 6 blocks. This should fit a double or queen-size bed. For a twin-size bed make 4 rows of 6 blocks.

Materials
5⅓ yards white fabric
8 yards red fabric
batting and backing material

Directions

Trace and transfer the pattern pieces to heavy paper to cut templates (see pages 18–19). Cut each fabric piece with a ¼-inch seam allowance. If you stay-stitch around each curved edge on the seam line, then clip to stitching before piecing, it will be easy to join pieces.

To make one block
Each block is 14 x 14 inches, and there are 36 blocks. The border is 3 inches wide.

There are two basic units in the Drunkard's Path design. A = a white convex shape #1 joined to a red concave shape #3, making a square. B = a red convex shape #2 joined to a white concave shape #4, making a square. In each block there are 8 A units and 8 B units. There will be a total of 288 A units and 288 B units in the finished quilt.

1. Make up all A and B units. Refer to #1 block diagram and piece 2 A units with 2 B units to make block C.
2. Refer to the diagram and you will see that C, D, E, and F are all identical but each one is placed in a different position to create the overall design.
3. Piece C and D together. Piece E and F together.
4. Join C, D with E, F to complete the block.

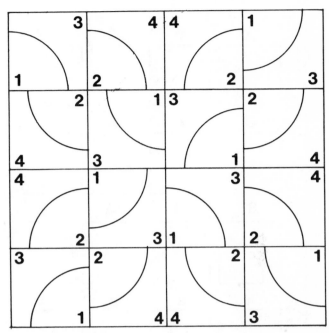

1. Block diagram

piece no.	in each block	in quilt
1 white convex	8	288
2 red convex	8	288
3 white concave	8	288
4 red concave	8	288

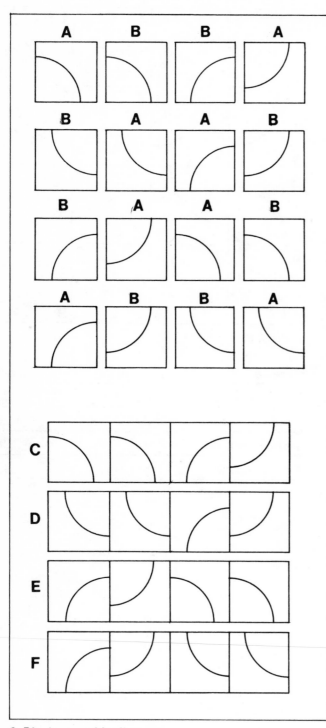

2. Block assembly diagram

Making borders

Cut 4 strips of red fabric 3½ x 92 inches. The corners on this quilt are mitered. They can be done this way or by overlapping (see page 20). Join top and bottom, then side strips.

Quilting

The quilting is done along evenly spaced diagonal lines across the top. Make a diagonal line from corner to corner, then mark from this line outward to each corner with approximately an inch between. For each line make a double line — for interest more than function.

Cut the backing material 2 inches larger than the quilt top. Baste the backing, batting, and top together.

Stitch along premarked lines with small running stitches. Another method for quilting is to stitch along all seam lines rather than along diagonally marked or grid lines.

To finish

Fold the backing to the front of the quilt. Turn the seam allowance under and blindstitch all edges to finish.

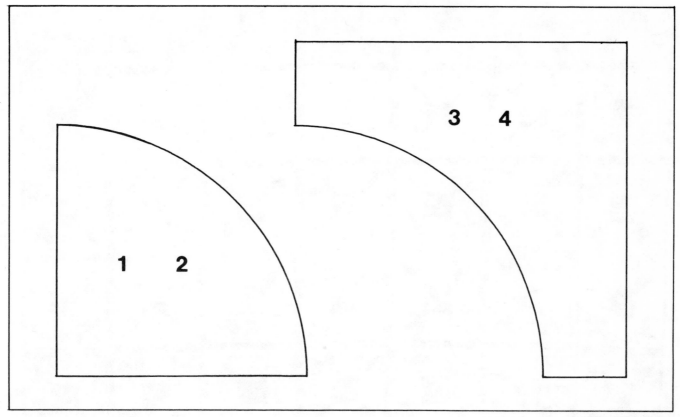

3. Pattern pieces

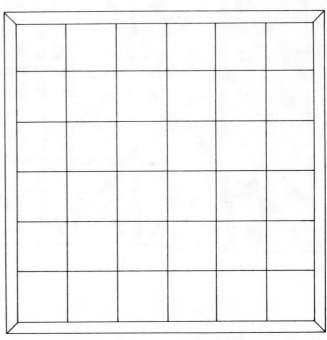

4. Quilt assembly diagram

Turkey Tracks

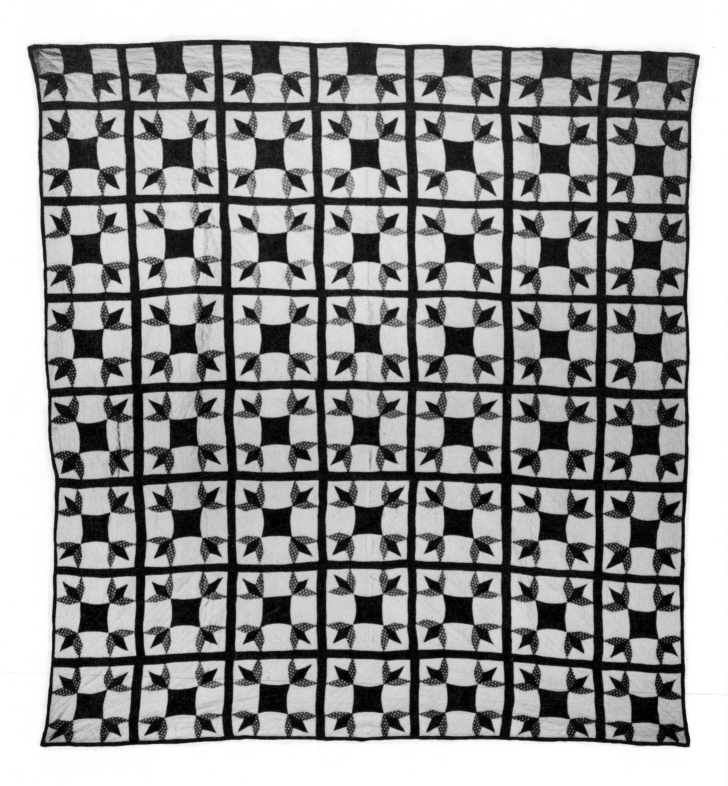

This quilt pattern was originally called Wandering Foot. However, brides refused to have a quilt with this pattern in their hope chests, fearing it would bring bad luck, and mothers would never have it on a child's bed for fear the child would leave. home, never to return. Thus the name was changed to the more popular Turkey Tracks.

Done in red, white, and blue, the bold blocks are framed with red sashes. The finished project is 89 x 98 inches, a good size for a double or queen-size bed. For twin size, reduce to 5 blocks across and 8 down. The top row of blocks here is actually made up of partial blocks, which you might want to make into complete ones. However, this section goes up and over the pillows or can hang down at the bottom of the bed, and probably won't be seen.

Materials

5⅓ yards red fabric
2 yards blue printed fabric
7⅔ yards white fabric (this fabric has tiny overall dots)
batting and backing material

Directions

Trace and transfer all pattern pieces to heavy paper for cutting templates (see pages 18–19). When cutting the fabric, add ¼-inch seam allowance. When piecing sections, refer to #4 quilt assembly diagram.

To make one block

There are 49 complete blocks and 7 partial blocks. Each complete block is 11 x 11 inches with 2-inch sashes between.
1. With right sides together and edges aligned, piece together a #1 with a #2 piece on either side to create the Turkey Track. Make 4 sets.
2. Cut a square of white fabric 11½ x 11½ inches.
3. Fold this square in half on the diagonal and press. Fold piece #3 in half on the diagonal and press. This will allow you to find the center of each in order to position the #3 on the background.
4. Turn seam allowance under on all edges of #3

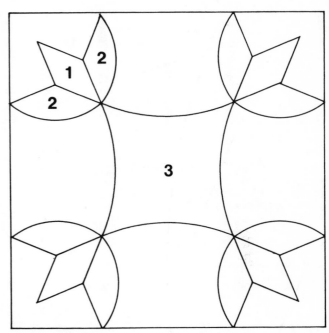

1. Block diagram

piece no.	in each block	in quilt
1	4	224
2	8	448
3	1	56

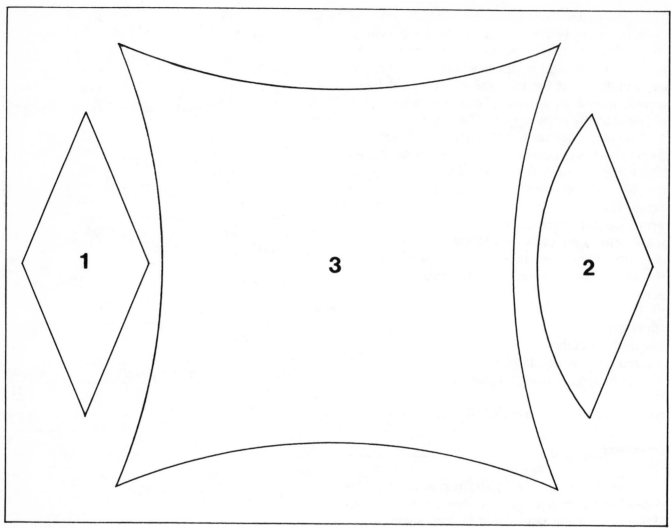

3. Pattern pieces

and press. If you are using cotton, it is easy to finger-press the edges. If not, you might want to stay-stitch along the seam line and then press under on this line. Blends do not crease as well as cotton and tend to spring back.

5. Pin #3 to the center of the block. Turn seam allowance under Turkey Track pieces in the same way. You might find it easier to use the template for turning edges under. Simply place the template on the back of the fabric and press edges over it. Remove and re-press seam allowance. Pin in position at each corner of #3.

6. Appliqué each piece by slip-stitching around edges.

Joining blocks

Each block is separated by a sash. Cut 6 strips of red fabric 2½ x 11½ inches for each row of 7 blocks.

1. With right sides together and edges matching, stitch the first sash to the right-hand side of a block. Open seam and press.

2. Repeat with each block and sash.

3. To join rows, cut 7 strips of red fabric 2½ x 89½ inches.

4. When joining rows, be sure to line up all seams from dividing sashes.

4. Quilt assembly diagram

Quilting

Although the background of the block is not heavily quilted here, you can certainly draw a grid on your material before basting and quilt along these lines after the backing, batting, and top are secured. The heart pattern (see page 44) would be a good design for the center of each block here.

All quilting on this project is done by taking small running stitches along each pieced and appliquéd seam line. Running stitches are done along the sash seams as well.

Begin by cutting the backing material and batting same size as the top. If you use the red fabric for the back, you can cut this 2 inches larger than the quilt.

To finish

Bring the extra fabric over to the top to finish the edges (see page 20). If you use a white fabric, cut to same size. Make a bias strip from the red fabric (see pages 21–22) and finish the edges as directed.

Robbing Peter to Pay Paul

The name of this quilt is often used to describe a positive/negative design. Every other block is the reverse color combination of dark and light. In this way it looks as though the pieces were taken from one block to make the next.

The inside border is red with a wider border of white. There is a thin band of red around the edges. The finished quilt is 86 x 96 inches, which will fit a queen-size bed. For a twin size, make 5 blocks across and 8 down.

Materials
5 yards red fabric
7½ yards white fabric
batting and backing material

Directions

Trace and transfer the pattern pieces to heavy paper for cutting templates (see pages 18–19). When cutting fabric pieces, leave ¼-inch seam allowance. Refer to the chart for number of pieces to cut from each color.

Each curved piece is joined with another curved piece. Before joining patches, see page 19 for preparing curved pieces.

To make one block
For piecing curved patches, you will have all pieces prepared accordingly. Each block is 10 x 10 inches. There are 56 blocks.
1. Refer to #1 block diagram for sequence of assembly. With right sides together, join a #4 red piece to each side of a #1 white center piece in the following way: Mark the center of each convex and concave piece. With right sides together and the outward curved piece #4 on top, pin together from the center points to one outer edge. Then pin from the center points to the other edge and stitch together. In this way the pieces will fit better and lie flat.
2. Using the reverse colors, join four #3 pieces to a center piece #2. Open all seams and press.

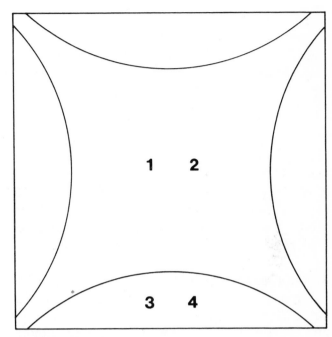

1. Block diagram

piece no.	in each block	in quilt
1 white centers	1	28
2 red centers	1	28
3 white sections	4	224
4 red sections	4	224

Joining blocks

This is a good project for quilt-as-you-go (see page 24), in which case you will add backing and batting and do the quilting of each block before joining. However, to make the quilt in the conventional manner, you make rows of blocks at this point.

1. With right sides together and edges aligned, join a white center block with a red center block. Alternate colors to make a row of 8 blocks.

2. When joining the rows, be sure that each row starts with a block in the reverse color of the one above it. Be sure that all seams line up when joining rows.

Joining inside borders

Cut 2 strips of red fabric 2½ x 80½ inches and 2 strips 2½ x 70½ inches. With right sides together and edges aligned, join side strips to front of quilt. Add top and bottom strips with overlapping corners (see page 20).

Making outside borders

Cut 2 strips of white fabric 6½ x 88 inches and 2 strips 6½ x 98 inches. Join with quilt as you did with the red border. There will be a little extra fabric, which you will trim when overlapping the corners (see page 20).

Marking for quilting

Trace and transfer the feathered pattern (see pages 90–91) around the outside wide border. Draw a diamond grid over all #3 and #4 pieces as well as over the inside border and white areas above and below the feathered pattern (see page 23).

To finish

Cut batting and backing same size as top of quilt and baste together. Quilt along premarked lines with tiny running stitches. If you use white thread, the flowers will show up on the red squares while the white squares will have a more subtle outline. This is a nice effect.

Cut strips of red fabric on the bias and make a continuous piece for binding the edges (see page 65).

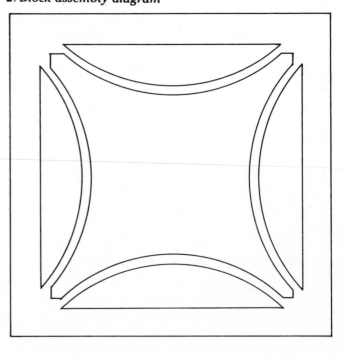

2. Block assembly diagram

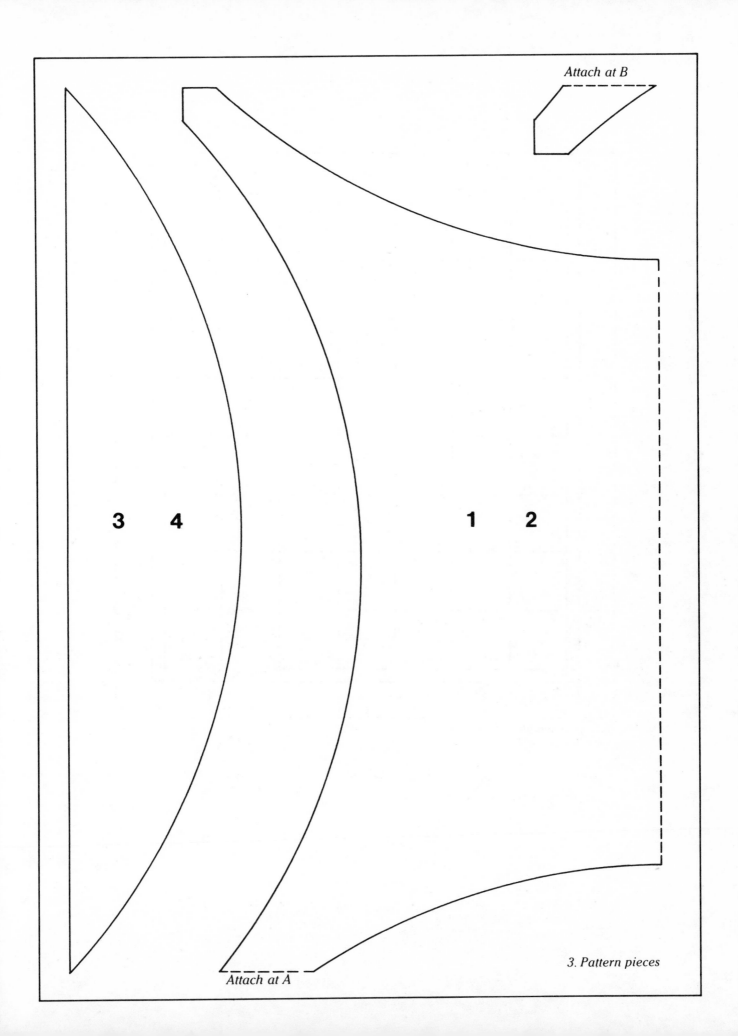

Attach at B

3 **4**

1 **2**

3. Pattern pieces

Attach at A

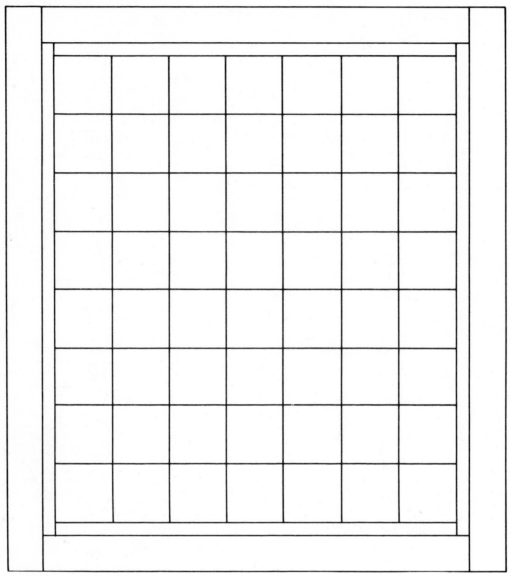

4. Quilt assembly diagram

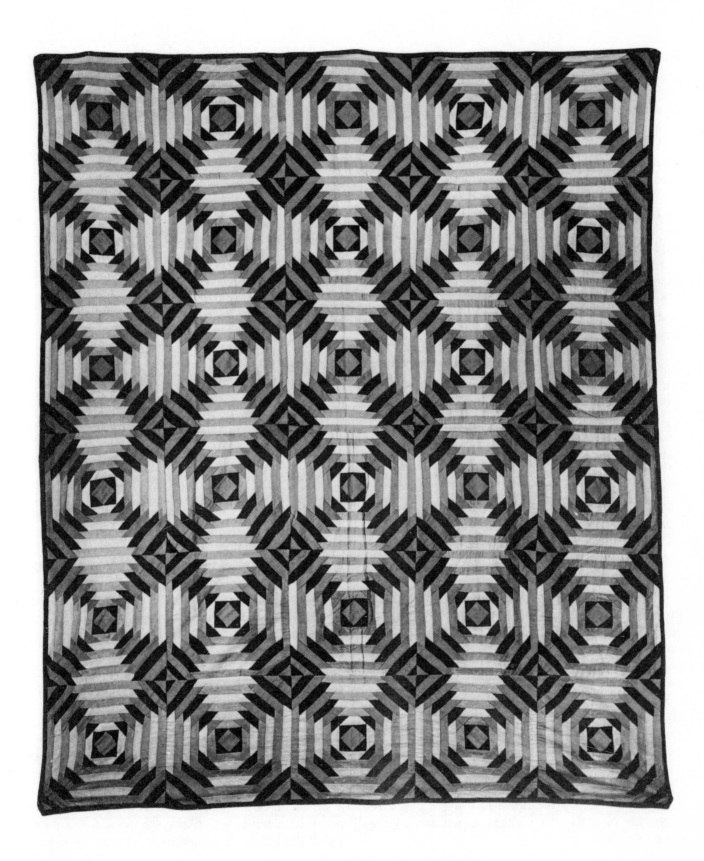

Quiltmakers all over the country have been making the Log Cabin design and its many variations since the beginning of quiltmaking. While it often looks intimidating to the beginner, it is a lot easier than it looks.

All Log Cabin patterns are built out from a center square with pieced logs that become progressively longer as they approach the edge of the block. The traditional Log Cabin designs are called courthouse steps, chimneys, off-center, and cornerstones. The Pineapple Log Cabin has trapezoid-shaped strips added to the center squares.

This quilt is 75 x 90 inches and is made up of 30 blocks. There are 5 across and 6 down, and each block is 15 x 15 inches. This will fit a double bed, and for a twin size, you make 4 blocks across and 6 down.

Materials
3 yards red fabric
3 yards tan fabric
3 yards blue fabric
3 yards black fabric
batting and backing material

Directions

The dramatic effect of this design is a result of using 2 light colors (tan and blue) and 2 dark colors (red and black).

The blocks are not identical. The color sequences are reversed so that when the blocks are put together correctly, a graphic pattern emerges. Refer to the chart for color positions for the full quilt layout. Diagram #4 shows you the positions of A and B blocks. The color plate will give you a better look at the block assembly.

Begin by cutting the number of pieces indicated on the chart for each pattern piece. Make a template (see page 17). Cut the fabric ¼ inch larger for seam allowances.

To make one block
1. With right sides together, join a #2 piece to each side of a #1 piece. Press seams away from the center.

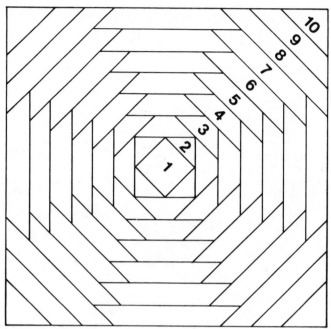

1. Block diagram

2. With right sides together, join a #3 tan piece to each side of the square.
3. Join a black #3 piece at each corner, as indicated on the diagram.
4. Add a blue piece #4 to each side of the new square and a red #4 piece to each corner, making a larger square.
5. Join tan pieces #5 on each side of square and black pieces #5 at each corner.
6. At this point you might want to press seams again. Always press away from the center.
7. Sew a blue piece #6 to each side of the piece just completed. Sew a red piece #6 at each corner between the blue pieces.
8. Continue to build the block in this way by adding the tan #7 pieces to each side, with a black #7 piece at each corner. Then add a blue #8 piece to each side, with a red #8 piece at each corner. Press seams toward the outside of the block.
9. Sew a black #9 piece to each corner only. Join a red #10 piece to the black #9 in each corner to finish the block. Press seams away from center.

piece no.	in each block	in quilt
1	1	30
2	4	120

piece no.	in each A block (15 blocks)	in quilt
3 (4 tan 4 black)	8	120
4 (4 red 4 blue)	8	120
5 (4 tan 4 black)	8	120
6 (4 red 4 blue)	8	120
7 (4 tan 4 black)	8	120
8 (4 red 4 blue)	8	120
9 (4 black)	4	60
10 (4 red)	4	60

piece no.	in each B block (15 blocks)	in quilt
3 (4 red 4 blue)	8	120
4 (4 tan 4 black)	8	120
5 (4 red 4 blue)	8	120
6 (4 tan 4 black)	8	120
7 (4 red 4 blue)	8	120
8 (4 tan 4 black)	8	120
9 (4 red)	4	60
10 (4 black)	4	60

Note: The A blocks and B blocks use a reverse color sequence. Be sure you make 15 of each. Refer to diagrams often when piecing, since the same size pieces are not always cut from the same fabric color.

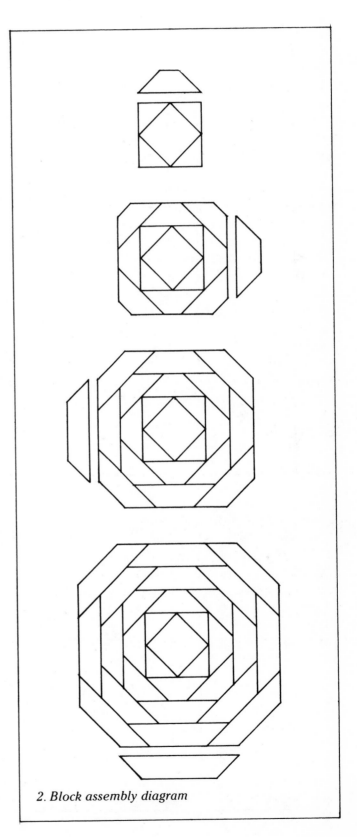

2. Block assembly diagram

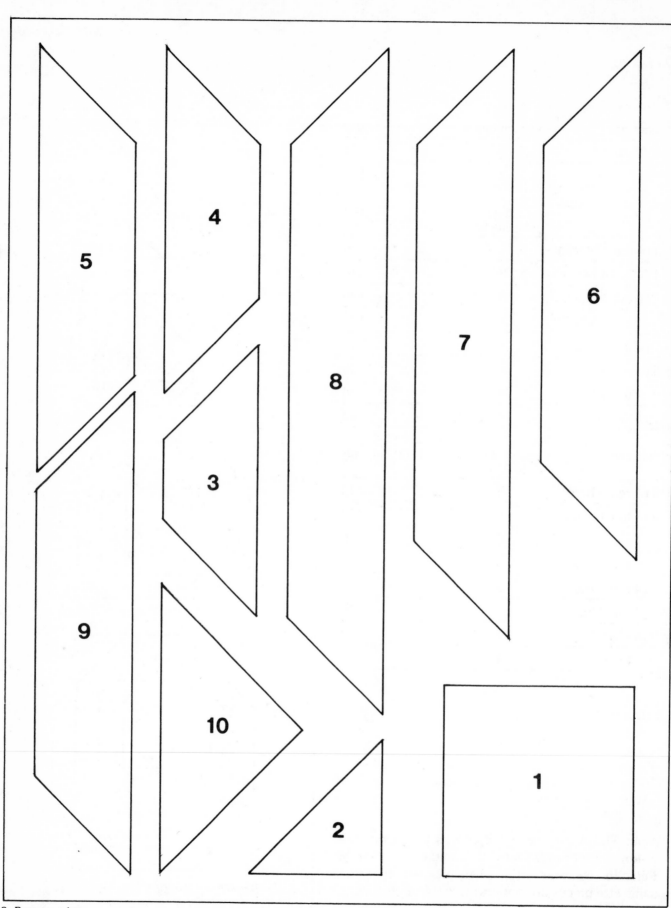

3. Pattern pieces

	B	A	B	A
B	A	B	A	B
A	B	A	B	A
B	A	B	A	B
A	B	A	B	A
B	A	B	A	B

4. Quilt assembly diagram

Joining blocks

With right sides together and edges aligned, stitch an A block to a B block. Continue to join alternating blocks to create a horizontal row of 5 blocks. Repeat to make 6 rows.

With right sides together be sure seams are matched between all blocks, and join rows to complete the quilt top. Press seams open.

Quilting

Since the quilting is done along the seam lines, no pattern is needed and you don't have to pre-mark the quilt.

1. Cut backing and batting same size as the top.
2. Baste top, batting, and backing together. If you take long stitches with white thread, you will be able to find them easily and cut them away as you quilt.
3. Take small running stitches on both sides of each seam of all pieces.

To finish

A bias strip of the black fabric is used here to finish the edges (see page 65). Finish edges as per directions on pages 21–22.

Log Cabin—Barn Raising

This is another variation on the familiar Log Cabin design. The basic block is called the spiraling log cabin. The diagonal split in shading is achieved by using darker prints of fabric on one half of the block and lighter prints on the other. In addition, the same print is used for pairs of logs that join at the corners.

This is an especially pretty color combination of warm-colored prints. When selecting fabric, you will need equal amounts of dark and light prints to create the dark and light pattern. As you can see, the overall pattern is imperfect. Some blocks are light where they should be dark. Often a quilt-maker would deliberately break the pattern in order to avoid inviting disaster for trying to imitate God's perfect work, a superstition that is, to this day, adhered to. When you come upon a perfectly symmetrical design with one obvious flaw, this is the reason.

This quilt is 70 x 105 inches and is made up of 8 blocks across and 10 down. It will fit a double or queen-size bed. For a twin size, make 6 blocks across and 10 down. Whether you add to or reduce the size of the quilt, it should always have an even number of blocks across to maintain the design.

Materials
6 yards assorted light prints
6 yards assorted dark prints
batting and backing material

Directions

Refer to the chart for the number of pattern pieces in each block.

Begin by tracing and transferring pattern pieces to heavy paper to cut a template (see pages 18–19). Cut each piece with ¼-inch seam allowance.

To make one block

Each block is 8¾ x 8¾ inches and there are 80 blocks. The pattern pieces will be joined in numerical sequence.

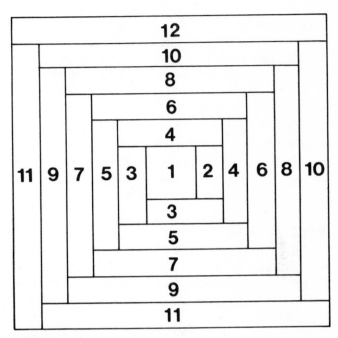

1. Block diagram

piece no.	in each block	in quilt
1	1	80
2	1	80
3	2	160
4	2	160
5	2	160
6	2	160
7	2	160
8	2	160
9	2	160
10	2	160
11	2	160
12	1	80

1. Each block begins with center piece #1 to which you will join a #2 piece to the right edge.

2. With right sides together and edges aligned, join a #3 piece to the bottom edge of #1 and #2.

3. To the left side of the unit join another #3 piece.

4. Join a #4 piece to the top of the unit and add another #4 piece to the side.

5. Continue joining each piece in numerical order as shown on block diagram #1 until block is complete. Press all seams away from the center.

Joining blocks

Once you have pieced all the required squares, you should refer to the diagram when assembling them. You want to be sure that the sequence is correct in order to create the overall pattern (see color plate).

With right sides together and edges aligned, join blocks to make horizontal rows of 8 blocks. Lay out the rows to be sure you have the pattern as it should be. Join each row, making sure that all seams are matched between blocks. Press seams open.

Quilting

Cut the backing and batting same size as the top and baste all 3 layers together.

There are various ways to quilt a Log Cabin quilt. Some quiltmakers suggest tying the quilt at each block intersection. This is a simple method for holding the backing, batting, and top together (see page 23). More ambitious quilters hand-stitch along all seam lines. Consider stitching along each block seam either by hand or by machine. This is also a good project for quilt-as-you-go (see page 24).

To finish

You can use any one of the three finishing methods (see pages 21–22). This quilt has a self binding trim of a ½-inch band of blue fabric with overlapping corners.

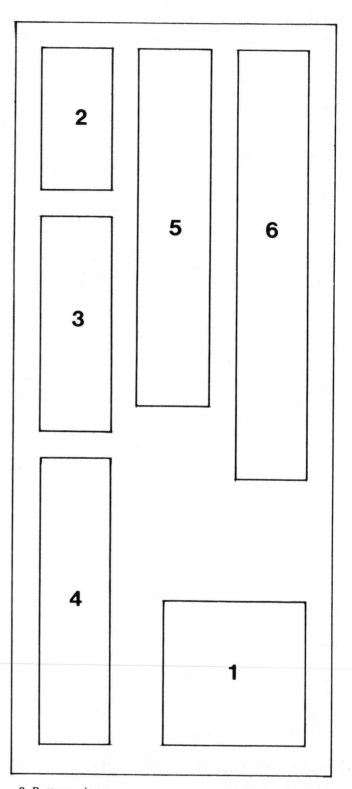

3. Pattern pieces

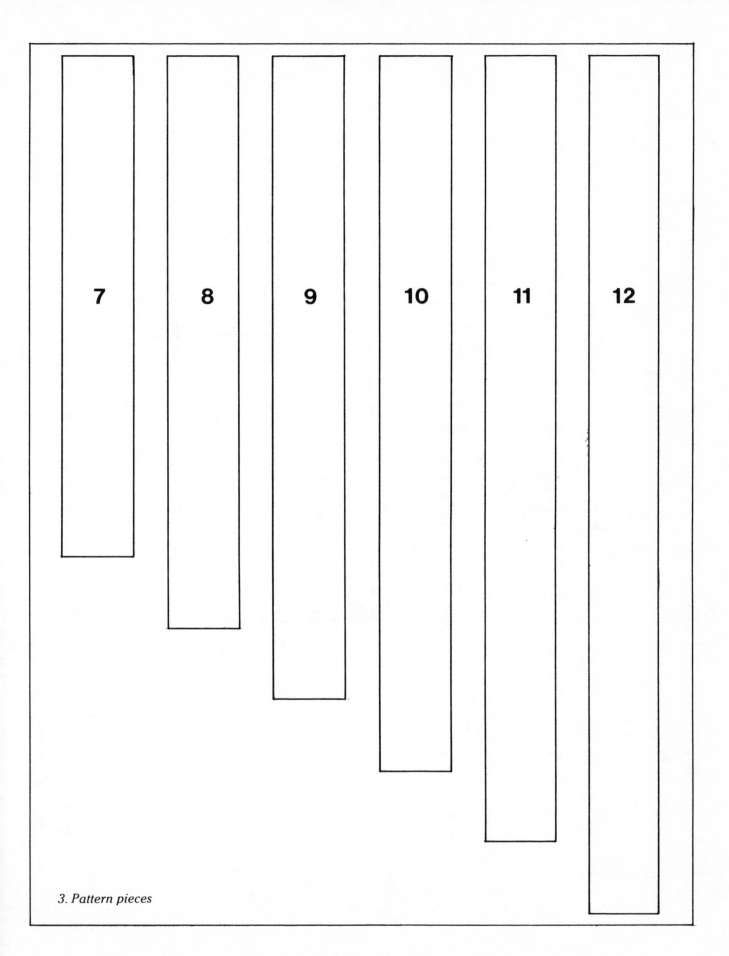

3. Pattern pieces

4. Quilt assembly diagram

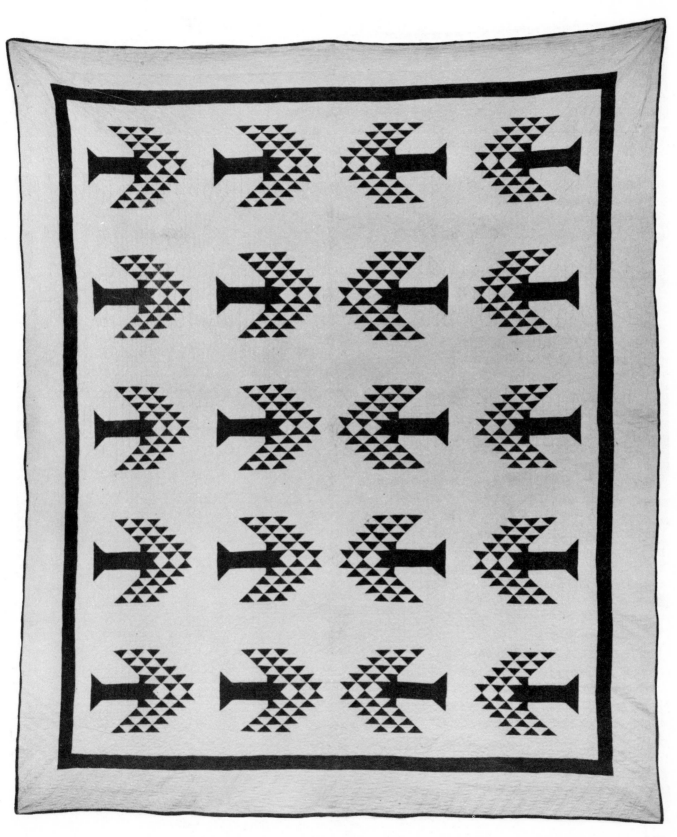

This is one of the most popular early-American quilt designs. You can see examples of it in many old quilts, usually with a brown trunk and printed green and brown fabric for the leaves. Symbolic of faith in eternal life, the design is a favorite in New England.

The finished quilt is 84 x 101 inches, which will fit a queen- or double-size bed.

Materials
2⅔ yards red fabric
9⅔ yards white fabric
batting and backing material

Directions

While this is a traditional design, one reason it looks contemporary is the use of white space around each bold design. It is made up of 20 pieced blocks, each of which is joined with a white block between. There are 12 quilted white blocks and 14 half blocks around the border with a quarter block at each corner.

Trace and transfer the pattern pieces to heavy paper for templates (see pages 18—19). Refer to the chart and cut the number of pieces indicated. When cutting fabric, add ¼-inch seam allowance.

Sometimes the directions for this design indicate piecing the triangle shapes, then appliquéing the trunk and pieced foliage to the background block. You may prefer to work this way. However, since there are no curved areas, only straight seams, the odd-shaped background pattern pieces are provided for piecing the entire block.

To make one block
Each block is 12 x 12 inches. You will begin by piecing each top half of the tree and then joining in the center.
1. Refer to diagram #2 for piecing sequence, and begin with a red triangle piece #1 joined to a white triangle piece #2. Alternating colors make 3 rows of 10 pieces. Join rows.
2. Repeat for opposite side of foliage. You will now have two pieced patches that are the same. Again

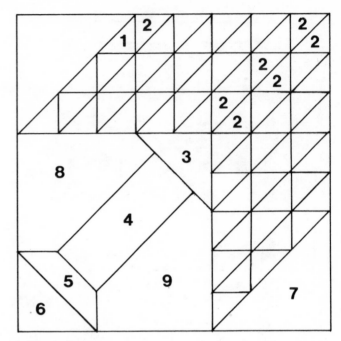

1. Block diagram

piece no.	in each block	in quilt
1	30	600
2	30	600
3	1	20
4	1	20
5	1	20
6	1	20
7	2	40
8	1	20
9	1	20

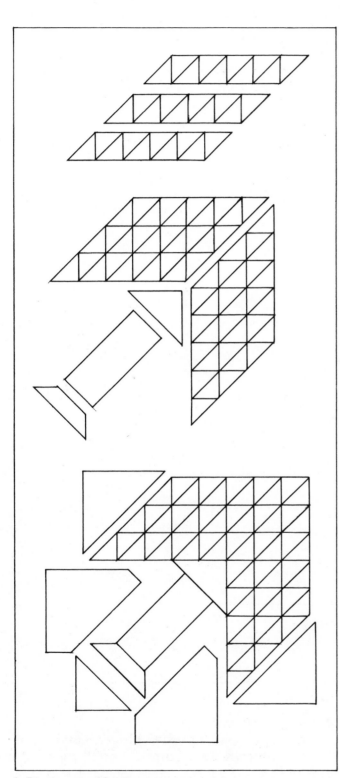

2. Block assembly diagram

refer to the diagram, and with right sides facing, stitch along seam line. The top of the tree is complete. Press all seams to the middle.

3. To make the trunk, fold piece #4 in half lengthwise and make a crease. Fold the triangle piece #3 in half and make a crease. This will give you the center of each piece. With right sides facing and center creases aligned, stitch across edge to join.

4. Join piece #5 to piece #4 as shown. Join trunk to tree top as indicated.

5. Join triangle piece #6 to #5.

6. Next join a #7 piece to either side of the tree to create the corners of the block.

7. With right sides facing and edges aligned, join top edges of pieces #8 and #9 to the foliage and then to the tree trunk. The block is complete.

Appliquéing trunk

If you prefer the appliqué method rather than piecing the entire block, follow the directions one through four.

1. Cut a square of white fabric 12½ x 12½ inches.

2. Turn all raw edges of pieced tree under ¼ inch and press.

3. Fold white block in half on the diagonal, and crease.

4. Center the tree (the crease is the guideline) and appliqué with small blind stitches.

Another appliqué method is to piece the tree as above and then piece each #7 triangle to the foliage. Then cut a white square of fabric 8 x 8 inches to join with the patched piece to which you will appliqué the trunk. This eliminates piecing #8 and #6.

Joining blocks

Cut 20 blocks 12½ x 12½ inches from the white fabric. Cut 7 blocks in half on the diagonal. Cut the remaining blocks in half and then in half again, forming 4 smaller triangles for each corner.

1. You will be joining blocks in rows. While you work, the pattern blocks will "read" on the diagonal. Refer to the photograph and join one small white triangle (corner piece) to the top of the first block.

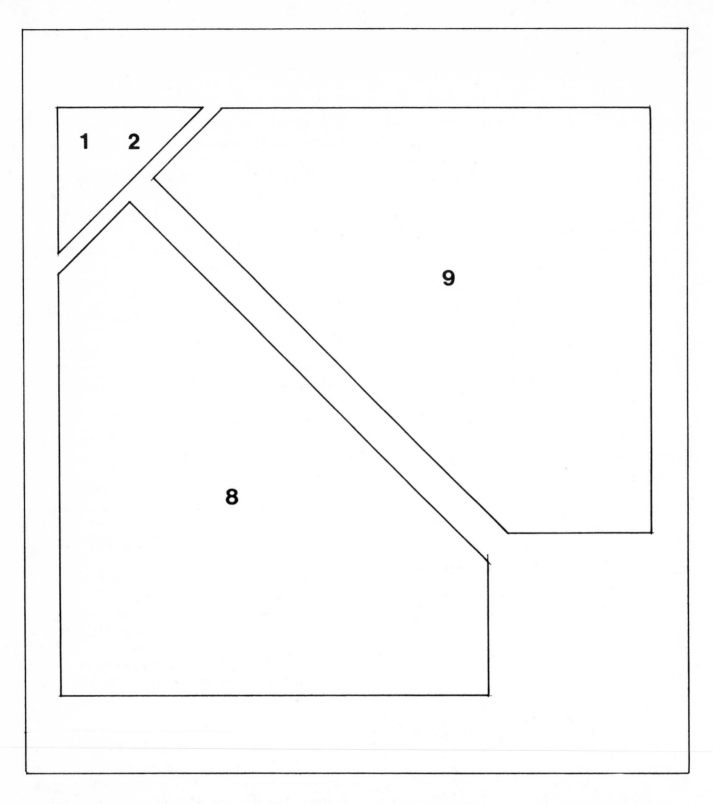

2. Join a half block (triangle) to one side of the block and another half block to the opposite side.
3. Continue to make rows of blocks according to the diagram. You will have 8 rows of blocks and half blocks (excluding the corner pieces).
4. With seams aligned, join rows in proper sequence. Open seams and press.

Joining borders

For the narrow red inside border, cut 2 strips 2½ x 78½ inches. Cut 2 strips 2½ x 94½ inches.
1. With right sides facing, place top border on quilt top with raw edges matching. Stitch across.
2. Repeat on the bottom edge of the quilt. Join side borders in the same way. Open seams and press.

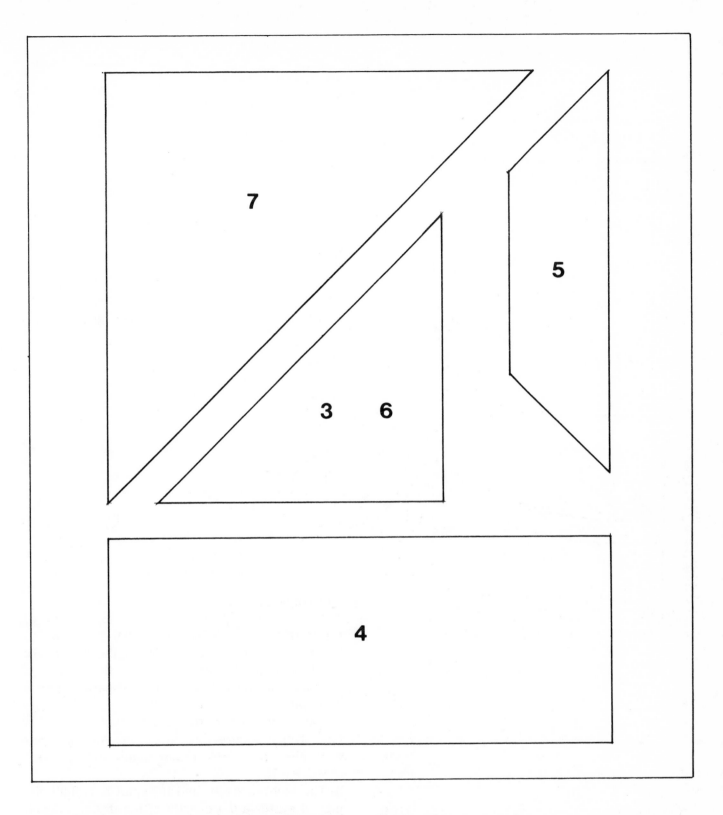

3. For outside borders, cut 2 strips 6½ x 86 inches and 2 strips 6½ x 92 inches from white fabric. This will give you a little extra length, which can be cut to fit after stitching. It's always a good idea to cut the border strips a little longer than the actual measure. It can always be cut down, but it's not so easy to add inches.

4. With right sides together, join side borders to quilt top. Add top and bottom borders last. This quilt has overlapping border corners (see page 20).

5. Quilting pattern

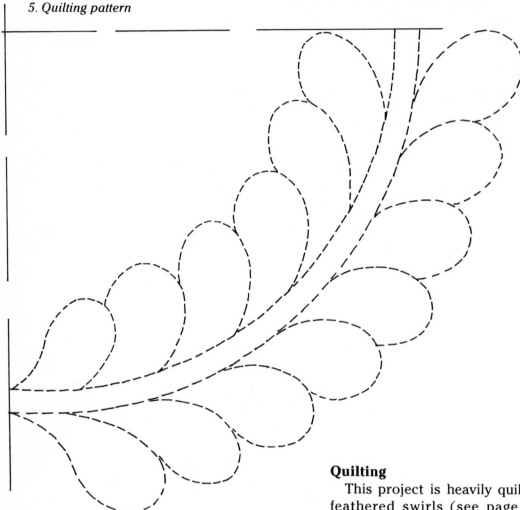

Quilting

This project is heavily quilted with a circle of feathered swirls (see page 150) in the white blocks, an evenly spaced grid on the patchwork blocks, and another grid pattern on the borders.

1. Trace and transfer the feathered pattern to the plain blocks.

2. Mark a grid across the patterned blocks so you have 1-inch squares. If you prefer, you can quilt each piece separately rather than creating a grid (see page 18).

3. The half blocks around the quilt have half circles of swirls and a quarter of the design in each corner triangle. Adjust the designs to fit.

4. Baste the backing, batting, and top together in a sunburst pattern (see page 23). The basting stitches will be cut away as the quilting progresses.

5. Take small running stitches where you have marked for quilting.

4. Quilt assembly diagram

To finish

The edge of this quilt is trimmed with a bias strip of the red fabric. It is one continuous piece that fits easily around each corner (see pages 21–22).

Feathered Star

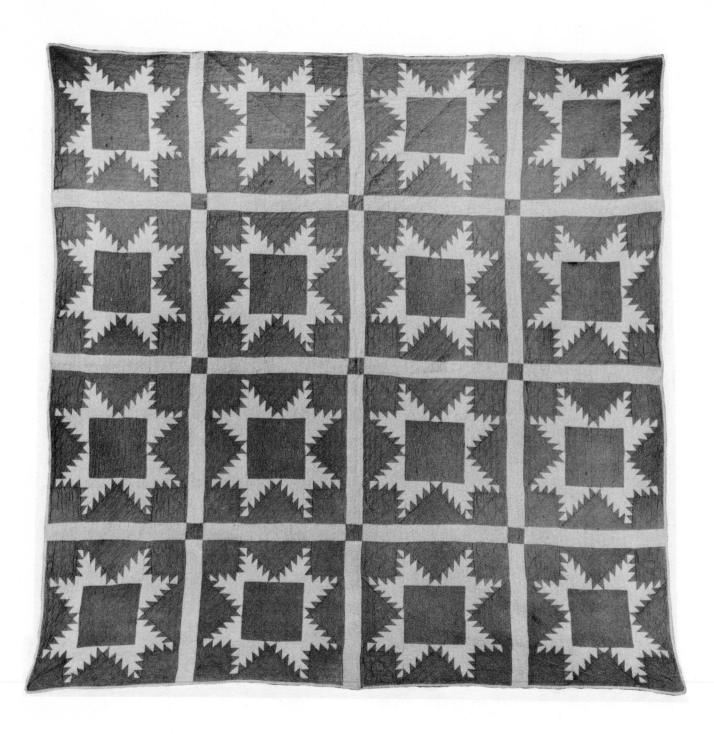

This quilt pattern is made up of many small triangle shapes pieced together in strips that are then joined to the center square. It will take patience and accuracy but is a lovely example of a 2-color pattern. This quilt is tangerine and white. It can be made in whatever colors match your room with the same dramatic effect.

This quilt is an 82½ x 82½ – inch wall hanging. If you would like it to fit a double or queen-size bed, make it with 4 blocks across and add another row of blocks for 5 rows. The finished quilt will measure 82½ x 105½ inches. For twin size use 5 rows of 3 blocks, which will make the finished quilt 60 x 100 inches.

Materials
6⅔ yards tangerine-color fabric
4 yards white fabric
batting and backing material

Directions

To make one block

Each block is 19½ x 19½ inches, and there are 16 blocks in this wall hanging.

Begin by tracing and transferring each pattern piece to heavy paper to cut templates (see pages 18–19). Adding ¼ inch for seam allowance, cut the number of pieces from each fabric as indicated on the chart.
1. Refer to block assembly diagram #2 when piecing the pattern. Piece 4 units each of A, B, C and D from #1, #2, and #3 pieces in the sequence indicated.
2. With right sides together and edges aligned, join eight #5 triangles around center square #4. Open seams and press.
3. Attach A units to #5 triangles and #4 square all ·around.
4. Attach B units to #5 all around.
5. Attach C units to #5 all around as indicated. *Note:* When adding each strip, it's important to keep referring to the diagram; as you will see, the piecing gets a bit complicated. It may be easier to follow visually than by just reading the directions.

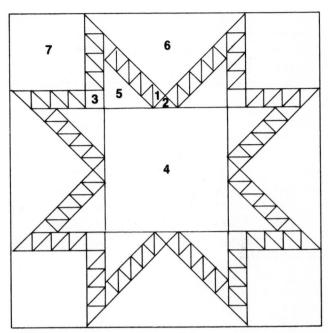

1. *Block diagram*

piece no.	in each block	in quilt
1	56	896
2	72	1152
3	4	64
4	1	16
5	8	128
6	4	64
7	4	64
sashes		
8 square orange		9
9 white strips		24

6. Attach D units to #5, side of #3, and edge of C unit all around. Your 8-pointed star is complete.

7. Piece four triangles #6 between units A and C all around.

8. Complete the block by piecing four #7 squares in each corner.

Joining blocks

Cut 24 strips of white fabric 2½ x 18½ inches. Cut 9 squares 2½ x 2½ inches for piecing the sashes.

1. With right sides together, join one strip to one side of a block. Continue to join blocks with sashes between so you have 4 separate strips of 4 blocks each.

2. Make 3 long sashes by piecing a #8 square between four #9 sash pieces. You will create 3 strips 78 inches long.

3. With right sides together, place the first strip on top of the bottom edge of a row of 4 blocks. Be sure seams are aligned before sewing together. Join all 4 rows in this way. Press open seams.

Quilting

Each square has a quilting pattern filling the space. Trace and transfer to these areas (see page 18). Next, trace and transfer border patterns. Each triangle #6 in the blocks is marked with a grid of double stitching lines.

Baste top, batting, and backing (cut 2 inches larger than top) together. Using small running stitches, quilt on either side of each seam line of each patched piece.

Stitch along all premarked quilting patterns.

To finish

Turn raw edge of backing forward ¼ inch and press. Fold over onto top of quilt and blindstitch to finish. This will create a thin white edging all around.

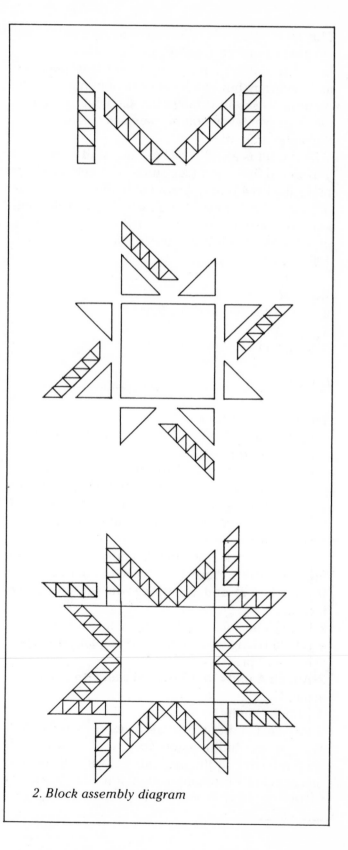

2. Block assembly diagram

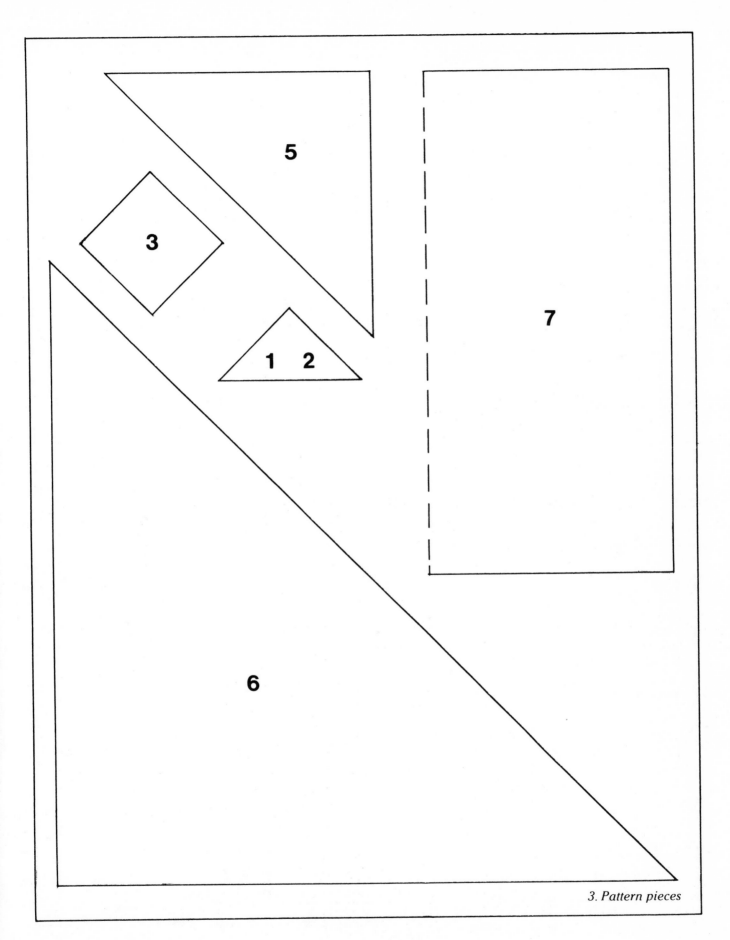

3. Pattern pieces

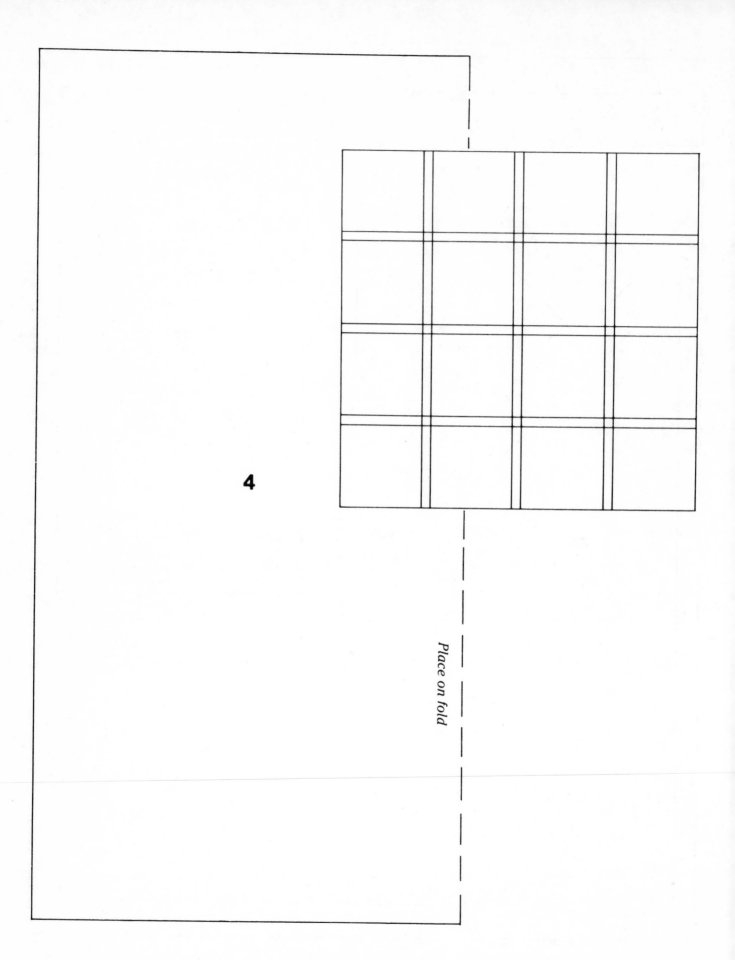

4

Place on fold

This is a very airy appliquéd quilt. Each block is divided by a white 5-inch-wide sash that is quilted in a different pattern than the blocks. There is a 6-inch-wide rose border all around.

While the blocks are divided so that two rows are set in one direction and two in the other, you might like to make the quilt with all blocks set in the same direction.

This is a single layer appliqué with edges overlapping. Therefore there isn't as much work involved as you might think. Only the outer edges are turned under on the rose. The stems can be made from bias fabric strips. The finished quilt is 87 x 87 inches.

Materials
⅓ yard orange fabric
5 yards green fabric
1 yard fuchsia fabric
1 yard pink fabric
7 yards white fabric
batting and backing material

Directions

All pattern pieces are same size needed, but you must add ¼ inch for seam allowance.

Trace and transfer patterns to heavy paper to cut templates (see pages 18–19). If you stay-stitch around each piece on the sewing line, it will be easier to turn the edges. However, if you're experienced at this, you may find that pressing the edges over the templates is all that's needed.

To make one block

Follow the layering sequence on diagram #2.
1. Cut a piece of white fabric 15½ x 15½ inches.
2. Turn under all edges of appliqué pieces that will not be lapped (refer to diagram), and press under. Before turning curved edges, clip inside seam allowance (see page 19 for more tips).
3. The easiest way to center the appliqué correctly is to make a full-size tracing of the rose pattern. Using the photograph or block diagram as a guide, trace each piece to make the full block. Place this over the white fabric, and slip each fabric piece

1. Block diagram

piece no.	in each block	in border	in quilt
1	1		16
2	1		16
3	1		16
4	1		16
5	5		80
6	1	23	39
7	1		16
8	1		16
9	1		16
10	1		16
11	1	26	42
12	2		32
13		4	4
14		4	4
15		23	23

under the paper to position. Remove the paper, pin the piece, then use the tracing each time you add a piece.

4. Start by pinning piece #4 to the center of the block. Add piece #3 on top of #4, followed by #2 and finally piece #1 in the center.

5. Before stitching the pieces to the background, pin piece #5 in position, lifting the edge of piece #4 to slip the base of the leaf (#5) under.

6. Position stem piece #8 with the base under the top edge of #4. Position leaf pieces #5 on either side and at the top of the stem so their bases slip under the stem.

7. When positioning stem piece #10 with #6 and #12, do the same. Join with #11, which will overlap the top of the bud #12.

8. Place piece #9 over #10 as shown, with the top edge under #4. Pin leaf piece #7 on stem #9, with the base under the stem.

9. Once all pieces are in position, you can slipstitch each appliqué.

Make 16 blocks.

Joining blocks

Cut sashes from white fabric 5½ x 15½ inches. You will need 12. Cut 3 long white strips 5½ x 75½ inches.

1. With right sides together, join one short sash to the right-hand side of the first block.

2. Continue to join blocks in this way, making 4 vertical rows of 4 blocks each.

3. Join all rows with the long sashes between.

Making borders

The appliqué for the border is a repeat pattern pieced in one curving continuous design. When you go around the corners, follow the guide, as you will have to piece #13 and #14 of the stem together.

1. Cut 4 white fabric strips 6½ x 90 inches. There will be extra fabric at each corner, which you will trim when overlapping corners.

2. Join top and bottom strips with right sides facing top of quilt and edges aligned. Open and press seams. Repeat at each side.

3. See pages 20−21 for mitering corners.

4. Position and pin each appliqué piece around the border as you did on each block. The border stems are piece #15, and each corner is made up of a #13 and #14.

Quilting

Mark diagonal lines across each block. The spacing is approximately 1 inch. The borders are quilted with a double line of stitching on diagonal lines 1½ inches apart. The border is quilted the same as the blocks.

Cut your batting and backing same size as the top, and baste all 3 layers together. When quilting with small running stitches, be sure to stop ½ inch before reaching the edges of the quilt.

To finish

Turn top and backing edges to the inside and press. If the batting extends to the seam allowance, trim it back to where the quilting ends. Slipstitch edges together for a self-finished edge.

4. Quilt assembly diagram

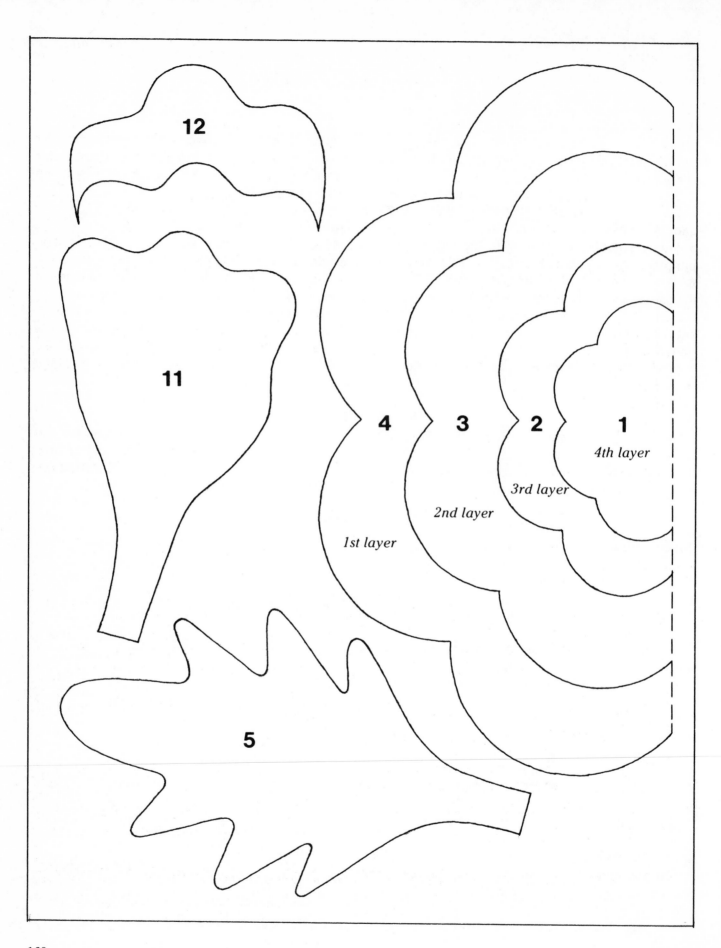

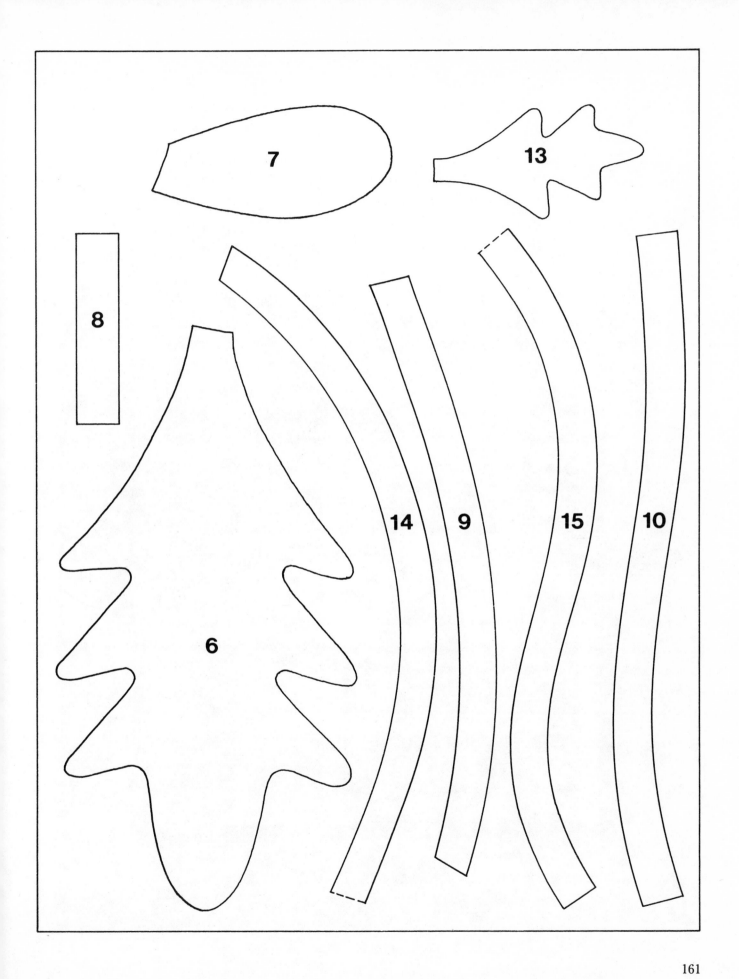

Alphabet Quilt

This is an interesting quilt that combines piecing and appliqué. You can use the alphabet letters, or you might like to personalize it with family names.

Each block is quilted in a diamond grid with the letters outlined in tiny contrasting stitches of white on red. The inside border has another quilting pattern of chevrons, and the outside border is done in the familiar swirls that look like intertwining ropes.

The finished quilt is 86 x 96 inches, which will fit a double or queen-size bed. To reduce the size for a twin, you will have to make the outside border smaller in width.

Materials
4 yards red fabric
3 yards navy blue fabric
⅓ yard yellow fabric
batting and backing material
white grease pencil or chalk
yardstick

Directions

Each letter must be enlarged (see page 18) before making your templates to cut the fabric (see pages 18–19). Since this is an appliqué design, you might find a ⅜-inch seam allowance easier to work with than the usual ¼ inch. Cut each letter and the corner sun patterns from red fabric (or solid color of your choice).

To make one block
Practically all the letters and the sun appliqués have curved or rounded areas. To prepare the appliqué, see page 20. Each block is 9 x 9 inches.
1. Cut a square of navy blue fabric 9½ x 9½ inches.
2. Center the appliqué on the fabric and pin in position.
3. Blindstitch the outer edge of the appliqué to the background fabric. You can do this on the inside edges as well, or, as was done here, use a decorative embroidery stitch for this area.

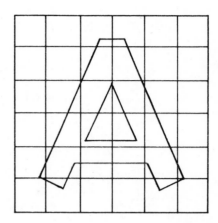

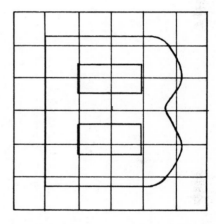

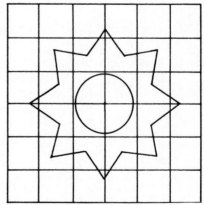

each square equals 1½"

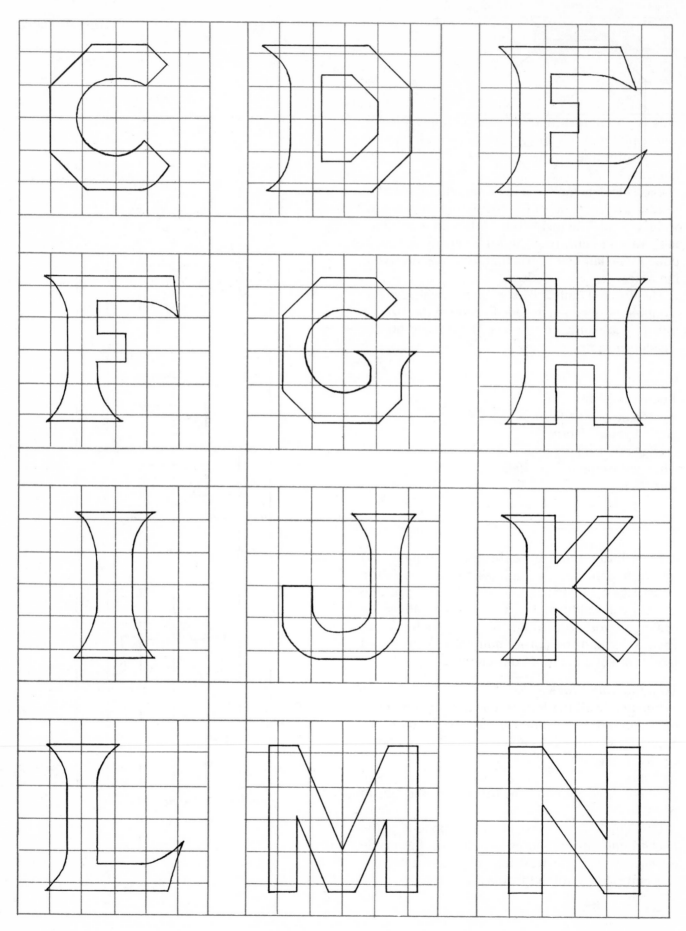

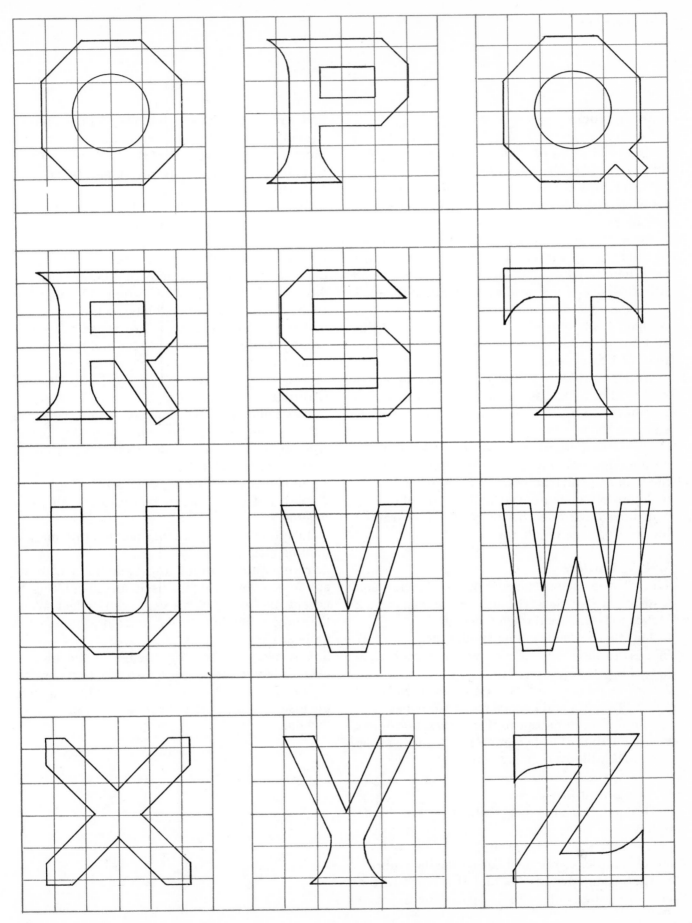

Joining blocks

The sashes framing each block are 2½ inches wide. Cut 71 strips of red fabric 3 x 9½ inches. Cut 42 squares of yellow fabric 3 x 3 inches.

1. With right sides together and edges aligned, join a sash to either side of the first block. Open seams and press.

2. Place the second block (going across from left to right) facedown on the first block so that the right-hand edge of the second block is aligned with the edge of the dividing sash. Stitch together along the edge.

3. Open seam and press. Continue to join blocks and sashes in this way until you have 6 horizontal rows of 5 blocks each.

4. With right sides together, join a yellow square to each end of a red sash. Continue to do this until you have a strip of 5 red sashes and 6 yellow squares. Make 7 strips.

5. Place a strip facedown on the first row of blocks so the edges are aligned. Be sure that seams are lined up and stitch across. Open and press.

6. Repeat on the bottom edge of the row of blocks. You now have one row of completely framed blocks. Continue to join rows in this way.

Making borders

1. Cut 2 strips of navy blue fabric 3 x 67 inches and 2 strips 3 x 78 inches. This will give you an extra 2 inches to be trimmed when finishing.

2. Join the top and bottom border strips (3 x 67 inches) to the quilt top and overlap corners (see page 20).

3. For the outside borders cut 2 strips of red fabric 10½ x 98 inches and 2 strips 10½ x 67 inches.

4. Join the shorter strips to the top and bottom as you did with the inside border. Join the side strips and finish with overlapping corners.

Marking quilt lines

This quilt has interesting quilting patterns in the different sections. You will need a white grease pencil or chalk from art-supply or needlework stores in order to see the lines on the dark fabric.

1. The inside navy blue border is marked with a chevron pattern of 3 evenly spaced lines. Trace and transfer the pattern to the border beginning at the corner of the first yellow square above the first block (not at the corner of the border). Continue to mark the border by retracing and transferring the pattern so it connects.

2. Using a yardstick, mark off diagonal lines across all sashes (not corner squares) and blocks (not appliqués). (See page 23 for easy method.)

3. Mark lines in the opposite direction to create diamonds on the blocks only (not border sashes).

4. Mark lines from corner to corner to form an X in each yellow square at sash intersections.

5. The outside border pattern repeats itself all around. Trace this from page 168 and transfer in a connecting pattern around red border.

Quilting

This quilt has a self-finished edge. Therefore, when doing your quilting, you must stop before reaching the edges in order to turn hems under. Leave ¼ to ½ inch free.

1. Cut backing and batting same size as top.

2. With batting between fabric, baste all three together.

3. Take tiny running stitches along all premarked quilting lines.

4. Hand-quilt around all seam lines of each appliqué. White thread, used for all quilting to accent the lines, gives a very pretty effect. When the thread matches the fabric color, the effect is more subtle.

5. Cut away all basting stiches. If the batting extends beyond the seam allowance, trim back.

6. Turn raw edges of the backing and top toward the inside of the quilt and slip-stitch or blindstitch together.

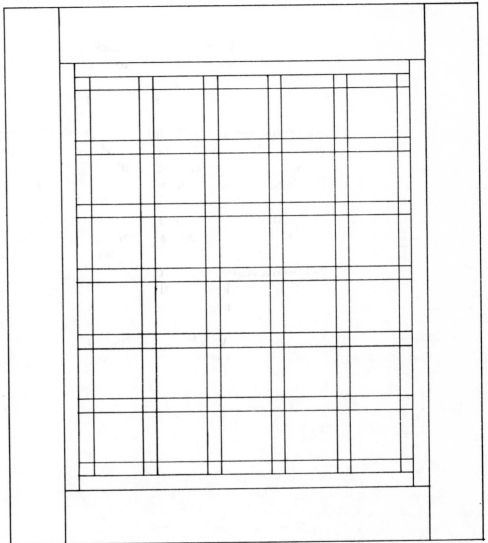

4. Quilt assembly diagram

Note: This quilt is a good quilt-as-you-go project (see page 24). You can make each block including the batting, backing, and quilting by hand or machine and then assemble with the borders, which you can also finish before attaching.

If you have a zigzag machine, consider this method for applying the appliqués. In this case you would not turn edges on each letter (see page 20 for machine appliqué).

To finish

See pages 21–22 for finishing edges.

This is another version of the Star of Bethlehem on page 100. Made in the traditionally American red, white, and blue colors, this one-patch quilt has no border blocks as does the other. The overall quilting is also much more extensive, and the background has a swirled feather pattern.

Materials

2⅓ yards red fabric
2⅓ yards blue fabric
5 yards white fabric
batting and backing material

Directions

Making the star

Since there are so many diamond shapes, a closely woven cotton is best for accurate folding of the points. To create the dramatic effect of this pattern, it is essential to cut and sew precisely. It is not a beginner's project.

Cut the border pieces first. Then cut diamonds from leftover fabric. In this way you will be sure to have one long, continuous piece for each side of the quilt. You will need 4 strips 2½ x 78½ inches of red fabric, 4 strips 2½ x 82½ inches of white fabric, and 4 strips 2½ x 86½ inches of blue fabric.

You might find it convenient to make 2 templates for cutting the diamonds. Use the pattern provided, which is the exact size of the finished patch without seam allowance. Trace and transfer to heavy paper (see pages 18–19). Next, add ¼-inch seam allowance to the traced diamond and transfer it to heavy paper. Cut out both templates and use the larger one to mark all fabric pieces. This is your cutting line. Place the smaller template on each diamond to mark the sewing line. This is double the work but will insure exactness when cutting and sewing. The finished quilt will reflect the extra preparation time taken.

Assembling patchwork

1. For each of the 8 larger diamond shapes that make up the points of the star, you will piece together 9 rows of 9 small diamond patches. Begin

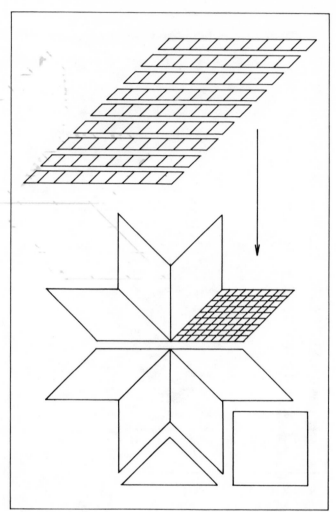

1. Block diagram

piece	in quilt
red	168
white	320
blue	160

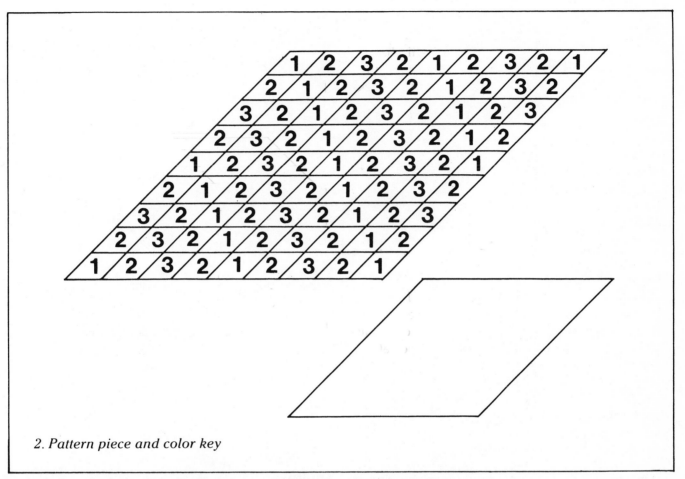

2. Pattern piece and color key

by placing a red piece facedown on a white piece. With edges aligned, stitch along one seam line to join. Open and press seams flat.

2. Refer to diagrams #1 and #2 and continue to make rows of 9 patches alternating with red, white, and blue (not always in that order). Check number sequence of color arrangement.

3. Join all points of the star. Align seams carefully.

4. Measure the length of each diamond side from the end point to where two sections are joined. It will be approximately 20 inches. From the white fabric, cut 4 squares to that dimension, adding ¼ inch to each side for seam allowance. Measure the same distance and cut 4 triangles to fit between the center points.

5. Join square pieces at each corner. Join triangles between points.

Joining borders

1. The border corners of this quilt overlap. However, you can miter them if you prefer (see pages 20–21).

2. With right sides together, stitch along raw edge of red border strip and white background fabric. Open and press on back and front of seam.

3. Join white strips followed by dark blue.

Marking quilt lines

Each section of this quilt is stitched in a different pattern. White thread is used throughout so you can see the tiny stitches on the red and blue fabric.

The grid on the border is made up of evenly spaced diagonal lines. Use a yardstick or metal ruler to mark the fabric (see pages 23 and 28–30).

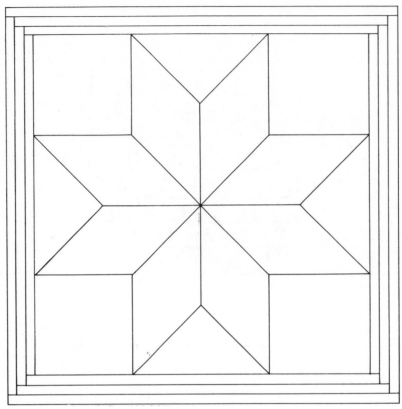

4. Quilt assembly diagram

The star patch is quilted in the same way. There are 3 parallel lines running across each row of 9 patches. The stitched lines meet in the center of the small red star.

The background is quilted with diamond shapes made up of parallel lines going in one direction and then the other.

Trace the swirling quilt pattern (see page 173) and transfer to the squares in the following way:
1. Divide the background square in half and find the center point. Divide each half in half again. Transfer the design to each section of the square to create a circular pattern.
2. When marking the triangles, divide each in half. Transfer the quilt pattern to one side of the triangle, beginning at the center bottom edge. Flip the design (tracing) over and transfer to the opposite side so the design is continuous. This will create a half circle of swirls.

Quilting

Baste quilt top, batting, and backing together. Be sure to cut backing 2 inches larger than the top. Quilting can be done on a machine or by hand. If stitching by hand, place each section in a large hoop or on a frame and take small running stitches along premarked quilting lines. Each stitch is approximately ⅛ inch apart. It is awkward to stitch such a large item on a sewing machine. If you prefer to do it this way, consider quilting as you go along (see page 24).

To finish

Fold excess material from the backing to the front of the quilt top. Turn the raw edge under ¼ inch and press. Blind-stitch to the top, covering the raw edge of the blue border. You will have a white trim approximately 1 inch wide all around the quilt.

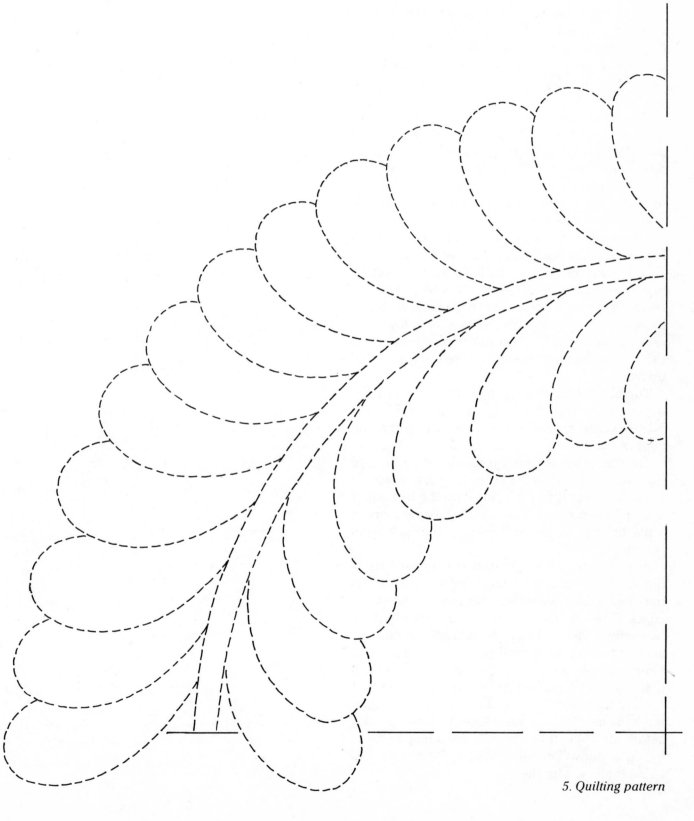

5. Quilting pattern

Quilt Care

To prolong the life of a quilt, it's important to care for it properly. To begin with, you should know something about the fabrics that were used to make your quilt. For example, some dark-colored fabrics, such as red or blue, may bleed when washed. For this reason it's a good idea to test the fabric when you are making the quilt. Some quilters don't take any chances and prewash all material to set the colors before beginning a project. In fact, there are those who prefer to dye plain cotton in order to create the exact colors desired. In this case many washings are necessary to remove all excess dye.

All the materials suggested for making the quilts in this book are washable. The finished quilts can be safely dry-cleaned as well. To wash a quilt by machine, use a mild detergent and a delicate cycle. Do not use bleach.When washing by hand, use a mild detergent and roll the quilt in towels to remove moisture. It's best not to wring it out, as this causes the stitches to weaken and possibly break.

Tumble-dry the quilt on a gentle cycle, or hang it out to dry with the weight evenly distributed. Place evenly spaced clothespins along the top edge of the quilt.

To iron, place the quilt facedown on a padded ironing board and steam-press the back. If storing the quilt rather than replacing it on the bed, roll it in a bed sheet rather than folding it. Never store in a plastic bag, as this will prevent the quilt from "breathing."

After several years' use a quilt may need some repairs. If the binding becomes frayed, it should be removed before adding another around the quilt's edges. Often quilting stitches break apart but can be easily repaired. Place the damaged section in an embroidery hoop and remove loose thread. Then restitch the area with matching thread. If patches need replacing, try to choose fabric that closely matches the original, and if necessary, wash the new fabric several times to fade the color before attaching it to the quilt. Bleaching some of the color out will create the faded effect needed to blend the new with the old.

Index